THE
CANADIAN MERCANTILE
ALMANAC
FOR
1846,

BEING THE SECOND AFTER LEAP YEAR.

CONTAINING, IN ADDITION TO THE INFORMATION USUALLY C
IN PUBLICATIONS OF ITS CLASS,

A GREAT VARIETY OF STATISTICAL A
OTHER USEFUL MATTER.

TORONTO:
PUBLISHED BY HUGH SCOBIE,
ADELAIDE BUILDINGS, KING STREET,

AND SOLD BY EASTWOOD & Co.
YONGE STREET.

"Rigo"

BURN'S
THMA
CURE

SKIN
CHEMIST
'N'S
DEALERS in Drug
Horse and
THIS REMEDY.

JOHN LABA
EXTRA
STOCK ALE
FOREIGN EXPORT
AWARDED
MEDALS
FRANCE
UNITED STATE
LONDON · CAN

"SPECTATOR" SUPPLEMENT.
THE "SPECTATOR"
CANADIAN
FARMERS' ALMANAC,
FOR THE YEAR OF OUR LORD
1867,

INSURANCE AGENCY,

r Leap Year, and until the
ar of the Reign of Her
Victoria.

ted to the Subscribers of
kly Spectator.

WHITE,
PUBLISHERS,
HAMILTON, C. W.

BOTTLES IN CANADA

Doris and Peter Unitt

Clock House

I

AN ORIGINAL CANADIAN PUBLICATION

First edition — limited to three thousand copies
Second edition — December 1973

BOTTLES IN CANADA

PUBLISHED by
Clock House, Peterborough, Ontario, Canada
Ⓒ Copyright 1972 by Doris and Peter Unitt

PRINTED IN CANADA by
Maxwell Review Ltd., Peterborough, Ontario

TO
DONALD MACKENZIE
MAC PROVICK
GEORGE CHOPPING
RAE MASSE
BILL HART
DAN MAC DONALD
HAROLD JARVIS
STEPHEN GIZA
AND
ALL THOSE
WHOSE KNOWLEDGE AND
ENTHUSIASTIC HELP
MADE THIS BOOK
POSSIBLE

Quart milk bottle from the Highclere Dairy believed to commemorate the historic meeting of Churchill and Roosevelt at Quebec City — Sept. 1944.

PREFACE

Realising the need for an across Canada bottle book and being inspired by the enthusiasm of Don Mackenzie, founder of the Bytown Bottle Club, we decided to produce "Bottles in Canada".

Contrary to our expectations this book has proved the most exciting of our ventures to date.

In researching bottle facts we have learned more of the history of the Canadian people than we discovered whilst researching either the Canadian pattern glass or the fruit jars and sealers. The bottle collector has on his shelves a more complete story of man. Bottles are universal, spanning the years, revealing the development of the nation, the social changes, the growth of industry, the superstitions and the gullibility of many people, the greed of the promoters with their strange and wonderful nostrums, of the long enjoyed bottle of beer, and the coming full cycle to show how little man has changed.

Bottles in Canada date back to the days of the early explorers. History records that the Spaniards visited British Columbia as early as 1592 and collectors on the West coast dream of bottles from Spain. In the Maritimes and Quebec collectors hope to discover fine old French bottles of the 17th century. It is known that the traders gave the Indians "fire-water" or as some called it "French milk" in exchange for furs. About 1660 Francois de Laval, first Bishop of Quebec, returned to France and begged the King, Louis XIV to put an end to the brandy traffic.

The story of glass making in Canada is short in comparison to that of other glass producing countries, and yet perhaps not as short as we have come to believe. In "A Guide to Early Canadian Glass" by Hilda and Kelvin Spence mention is made of medicine vials of the period prior to 1787. A photograph (Plate 1) shows how fragile they were. The origin of these vials is not proven, but it is possible that they were the first Canadian made glass containers.

Nineteenth century whiskey jug, still in its wicker basket.

Bottle collecting can mean family outings in search of old homesteads long abandoned and the finding of early medicinals, spirit bottles and early food containers. It can mean a joyful group of skin divers discovering an old wreck with a number of lovely blown bottles there for the bringing ashore or maybe it can mean a six month search along the coast line near Halifax by two divers determined to gather all the known James Roue bottles. It can mean an ardent collector and three boys digging out a dump that has been closed for nearly fifty years and disclosing bottles by the hundred. It takes the form of enthusiasts who save all their "Avons", or their blue milk of magnesias or bromos, searching for other blues at flea markets and in stores.

It can also mean two researchers in pursuit of photographs and facts becoming charmed by the friendly, happy collectors and their fascinating collections and ending up with a growing array of interesting bottles.

The aspects of bottle collecting are staggering in their variety. In this volume we show some small part of what has been found across Canada at this time, it is but a fraction of what still remains to be discovered.

We hope the bottle collector will continue to track down the history of the bottles he finds and share his knowledge with others, for in so doing he will add immeasurably to the wealth of Canadian heritage.

Doris and Peter Unitt,
Peterborough,
Ontario, Canada.
April, 1972.

Clock House

Chestnut bottle, 18½ in. high. Excellent example of whittle marking.

YE STUFF

INDEX

Bottles actual size.   *Authors' collection*

An 1867 – 68 Hamilton Directory Advertisement shows: R.A. Pilgrim, Steam Soda Water Manufacturer,
Corner of King and Cathcart Streets, Hamilton C.W.

ACKNOWLEDGEMENTS

An adequate 'thank you' for all the help and encouragement we have been given during the planning and preparation of BOTTLES IN CANADA can best be said by showing the results.

Everywhere we travelled collectors opened their doors and made us welcome; we were permitted to take photographs, sometimes at very early or late hours to fit in with work schedules.

Treasured documents were loaned to us, catalogues and old books were checked for facts. Librarians searched through early directories, readers of the Ontario Showcase provided us with almanacs and early catalogues; newspapers which had almost disintegrated were proffered by some enthusiasts and valuable information was brought to light.

It would not be possible to mention everyone, but special appreciation is due to the following:

Mr & Mrs Dave Audet,	Stanstead,	Que.
Mrs Olga Audet,	Stanstead,	Que.
Molly & George Beckner,	Hamilton,	Ont.
Mr & Mrs Albert Book,	Hamilton,	Ont.
The Book Boutique,	Ottawa,	Ont.
Mr & Mrs R.J. Burgess	Hamilton,	Ont.
Mrs Dennis Campion,	Lyndale,	P.E.I.
Dianne Carrol,	Hamilton,	Ont
Mr & Mrs G. Chopping,	Esterhazy,	Sask.
Anne & Hugh Collens,	Hamilton,	Ont.
Cook's Antiques,	Hartland,	N.B.
Mr H. Drinkwater,	Hudson,	Que.
Mr & Mrs K.G. Farrell	Ottawa,	Ont.
Vera & Allen Fraser,	Pike Bay,	Ont.
Nora Goodall,	Vancouver,	B.C.
Stephen Giza,	Halifax,	N.S.
Mr & Mrs Larry Griffin,	Peterboro'	Ont.
Mary & Bill Hart	Seaforth,	Ont.
Mr & Mrs G. Hazard,	Fallbrook,	Ont.
Elisha & George Hicks,	Listowel,	Ont.
Bill & Dolly Hodd,	Hamilton,	Ont.
Mr & Mrs Harold Jarvis,	Grimsby,	Ont.
Mr & Mrs Barry Hum,	Peterboro'	Ont.
Hunques & Junques,	Madoc,	Ont.
Mr Dave Kay,	Cranbrook,	B.C.
Mr D. Haig Leckie,	Hamilton,	Ont.
Donald Mackenzie,	Ottawa,	Ont.
Mr & Mrs Colin MacLeod,	Lennoxville,	Que.
Mr & Mrs D. MacDonald,	Moncton,	N.B.
Mr & Mrs J. MacDonald,	Moncton,	N.B.
Kaye McFarland,	Napanee,	Ont.
Mary McGill,	Hamilton,	Ont.
Betty Mitchell,	Chatham,	Ont.
Jim Murphy,	Halifax,	N.S.
Mr Jack Noy,	Toronto,	Ont.
Betty Pedderson,	Hamilton,	Ont.
Mr & Mrs Len Pope,	Baldwin,	Ont.
Mr & Mrs Mac Provick,	Esterhazy,	Sask.
Radone's Antiques,	Amherst,	N.S.
Bruce Richardson,	Orillia,	Ont.
Jack Rogers,	Peterboro',	Ont.
Mrs M. Rosborough,	Peterboro',	Ont.
Mary & Judy Sherb,	Hamilton,	Ont.
Miss Helen Smith,	Barrie,	Ont.
Dick & Margaret Smythe,	Hamilton,	Ont.
David Staffen,	Seaforth,	Ont.
Sandy Stewart,	Peterboro',	Ont.
Mr & Mrs D. Stuart,	West Brome,	Que.
Mr & Mrs D. Unitt,	Orillia,	Ont.
Rosemary Unitt,	Ottawa,	Ont.
Mr & Mrs J Welbourne,	Peterboro',	Ont.
Charles Williamson,	Omemee,	Ont.
Colin & Graeme Young,	Seaforth,	Ont.

Bottles actual size.

Authors' collection.

An 1867 — 68 Hamilton Directory Advertisement shows: H.W. Bilton, Wholesale Manufacturer of Soda Water, Sarsaparilla and Lemon Pop, Depot No. 9, King Street West, Hamilton. C.W.

We were greatly assisted in our research by:

Gwen Findlay, Editor, Review Weekly, Peterborough.

Miss Katharine Greenfield, Hamilton Public Library.

Miss Janet Holmes, Royal Ontario Museum, Toronto.

Mr Rae Masse, Fort Steele Historic Museum, B.C.

Mrs H. Matthews, Hamilton Spectator Library.

Mrs Carole MacKaay, Assistant Archivist, Molson's Brewery.

Members of the Parkland Bottle Club, Saskatchewan.

The Staff of Peterborough Public Library.

We would also like to say thank you for a job well done to the staff at Maxwell Review Ltd. and Colour Reproductions Ltd., Peterborough, Ontario.

Doris and Peter Unitt,
April, 1972.

The photograph on Page 111 was taken by Bob Brady and reprinted by permission of the Huron Expositor, Egmondville, Ontario.

Pages 185 — 193 were reprinted from "Treasury of Canadian Glass" by permission of Clock House, Peterborough, Ontario.

Very large glass drug store bottle from the Bill Hart collection.

OLD BOTTLES

Originally bottles were made from animal skins, gourds, shells, animal horns or hollowed wood. Anything that could serve as a container was used.

Wine was made by man very early in his development and stored in goat skins, one leg was allowed to project from the skin and served as a spout. Skin bottles are still used by people in some parts of Asia.

African and Chinese artists made beautiful bottles from gourds, many were elaborately carved and colourfully decorated, even the wooden stoppers were carved with most intricate designs.

Canadian Esquimaux and Indians made vessels from woven spruce, tamarack or willow roots.

Stoppers were made of anything which would prevent the contents from spilling Many things served this purpose: woven reeds, blobs of clay, shaped bones, wedges of wood, rolled strips of linen were used by the Egyptians to close their jugs and a large dab of pitch was used as a seal. A mark was sometimes added to the seal to show ownership and this custom was used on bottles of the 17th century in England and France. Some of these bottles were brought to the Americas by the early adventurers. Woven or braided grass has acted well as a stopper and the corn cob has sealed many a jug of liquor. Cork was discovered about 600 B.C. and used by the Greeks and Romans.

It is doubtful if any glass or pottery bottles were produced in Canada on a commercial basis until the early 19th century. Little evidence has yet been found to suggest that any factory existed prior to 1800.

Bottles were imported from England, Ireland and America for the use of the druggists, brewers and distillers.

One of the most interesting bottles in Canada is the Royal Ontario Museum's "New Year bottle", fashioned in ancient Egypt about 600 B.C. This bottle is made of hard glossy faience, which is fine powdered quartz mixed with vitreous glaze. The body of the vessel is then coated with a glaze, coloured by adding a copper compound. The bottle in the Museum has lost its brightness and is now a faded green. The mouth and convex sides of the bottle were made separately and joined together by a band before firing and finishing. This lovely example from the past is 6½ in. high and lentoid in shape, it is inscribed with the traditional New Year greetings of the Egyptians. A monkey sits on each shoulder below the flared lip.

Two of the earliest bottles so far known in Nova Scotia are the Louisburg bottles in the Nova Scotia Museum, these are French liquor bottles of about 1740. The same type of bottle has been found in other parts of Canada.

from "The Manufacture of Glass".

Blowing the ball for a glass cylinder.

These antique engravings show men and boys at work in an early glass factory.

BRIEF DESCRIPTION OF EARLY BOTTLE MAKING

1. Gob of molten glass is gathered from furnace using blowpipe.

2. After a few puffs it is rolled gently (marvered) on table, still continuing the blowing.

3. Swung to elongate, if it is to be free-blown. Shaped and finished with pontil or push-up tool.

4. If mold is used the 'parison' is lowered into mold and blowing continued until glass touches all sides of mold.

5. Removing bottle from mold the server takes it to the gaffer who is seated near a small furnace, known as the 'glory-hole.' The pontil rod is applied to the bottom and the server holds the bottle by this while the gaffer finishes the neck and lip. The server gently rotates bottle during finishing process. The bottle is then removed from the pontil rod.

6. Bottles are placed in the 'lehr' for cooling. This process is called annealing.

PONTIL MARKS

A pontil mark is a round jagged scar left by the breaking off from the tool (pontil rod) of the completed bottle after the neck and lip of the bottle had been finished.

Some bottles have the pontil scar ground off or melted into a smooth blob. The blob type of mark is found on old black bottles.

The ground pontil mark is usually on the more decorative and costly bottle.

The majority of those found with any of the three types of mark are old, but careful consideration must be given to the origin of the bottle. Imports from Europe and Mexico with pontil marks can be and often are of recent manufacture.

Pontil mark on jeroboam.

Left — Early blown bottles are completely individual. Note the variations in the push-up. The date given for these bottles is pre-1860. The practice of making bottles in this manner is still followed by some firms for special orders. A push-up type bottle with laid on lip was offered in a Canadian glass company catalogue of the early 1900's.

Right — Small blown flasks with flared lips. Pontil marks can be clearly seen. Note the variations in the basic shape.

Left — Later bottles are more uniform. These four are early machine made types, as shown in Dominion Glass Company's Catalogues Nos. 8 and 9.

Left — Neck of blown bottle. Note bubbles & imperfections.

Right — The seam around this bottle shows that a cup-mold was used in the making. Note the smoother finish.

Seams indicate the method used in the manufacturing of bottles. The earliest bottles were free-blown therefore they were without seams. The Romans and Syrians were experts at mold making and fashioned them in clay, wood and metal.

The glass blower makes a bottle by taking a gather or gob of molten glass onto his blow-pipe and after a few puffs places the gather into the mold. He continues rythmic puffing until the gather touches the mold all round, he then stops blowing. The molds were made in sections and when the bottle was removed the seam was plainly visible.

Early molds were used for the formation of the body or lower bottle, the shoulder and lip being added later. Thus each bottle varied from the next and some were crooked.

With the coming of the 'closed mold', bottles came from the mold complete and uniformity of shape and size was the result.

Push up base of early blown bottle. Every bottle of this type has character.

Three cylinder blown bottles, with laid on lips and push up bases. Tallest bottle is 13 in., this bottle has D.B. sand blasted on its base.

21

LIPS COME IN ALL STYLES

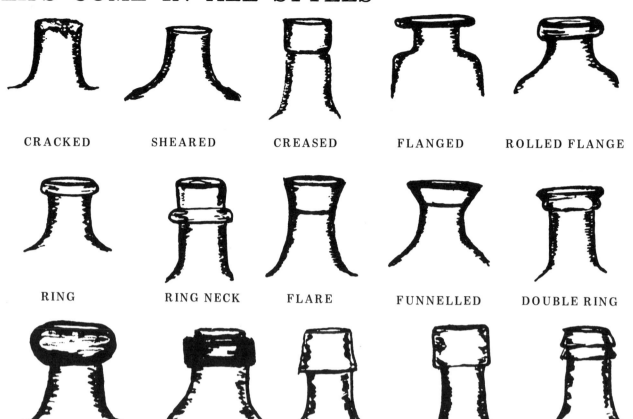

CRACKED   SHEARED   CREASED   FLANGED   ROLLED FLANGE

RING   RING NECK   FLARE   FUNNELLED   DOUBLE RING

BLOB TOP   APPLIED LIP   CASTOR OIL   CORK   EARLY APPLIED LIP

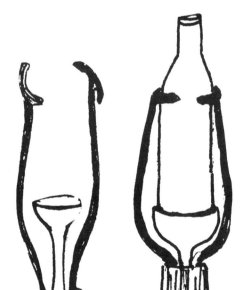

SNAPCASE c.1850
The Snapcase was invented around 1850 and is described as a case which held the bottle while it was being finished. The tool was simi-

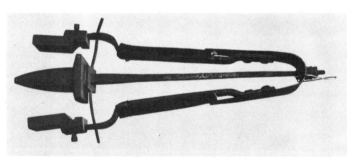

Hand operated lipping tool. Date stamped on handle - 1856.

lar to the drawing shown and used by bottle making firms such as the Hamilton and the Burlington glass factories.

This finishing tool remained in use until the 1880's, eliminating the pontil mark and thus dating the majority of free blown bottles as prior to 1860.

Some European firms continue to use the old glass blowing methods to produce bottles for fine quality wines and liqueurs. Mexican glass blowers are also making bottles in the early manner.

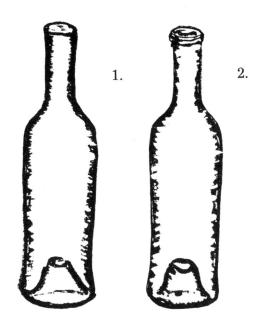

1. 2.

When using the seam as a date guide it is as well to remember that it is a general guide and not infallible. Other aspects have to be taken into consideration. The method of finishing can obliterate some of the seam or mold marks. Uniformity of the finished bottle should be noted and thickness of glass is another factor to study.

Older methods of making bottles were in use in Canada for a longer period than in the United States. The Owens Automatic Machine was not in general use here until 1913 and some glass works did not become fully automated until 1920. Cylinder blown bottles are listed in Canadian catalogues of the 1900's.

KEY TO DRAWINGS

1. Free-blown, sheared lip. Pre-1840.

2. Free-blown, laid on lip. Pre-1860.

3. Turn mold. This obliterated seam marks, but left faint circular scratches. 1880-1890.

4. Cup mold. Many of the beautiful black bottles of the 1760 - 1860 period were made in this type of mold.

5. Three piece mold. There were at least two types of three piece mold, the one shown here and the three piece leaf mold. Bottles of the latter type have the seam from top to bottom of the bottle, it was not however

3. 4. 5.

used on utilitarian types, but rather for the decorative and more costly bottle.
Both types in use 1870 - 1910.

6. Post bottom mold. Seam marks on bottles made in these molds continue in circle on base as well as showing up the sides. The bottle would be well balanced in shape, since the mold could be used combined with other types and the base plate was self centering. Period: 1820 - 1900.

7. Seam on lip usually indicates bottles made prior to 1903 if American and pre-1913 if Canadian.

8. Seam full length. After 1903, but remember the exceptions to the rule.

6. 7. 8.

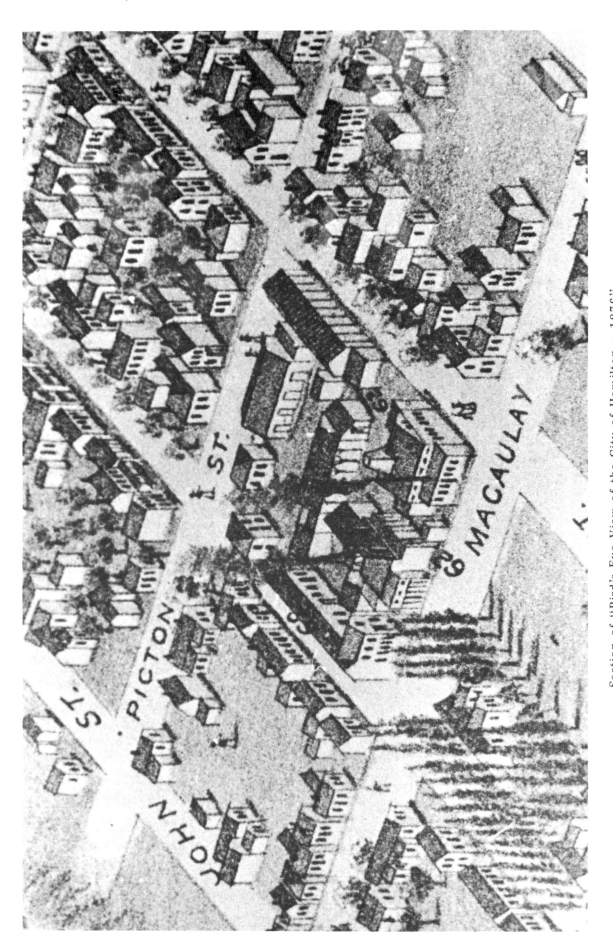

Section of "Bird's Eye View of the City of Hamilton — 1876" showing The Hamilton Glass Company's Works. No. 62 on map.

CANADIAN GLASS FACTORIES

ALBERTA

The Dominion Glass Co., Ltd., Redcliff.	1913 -

BRITISH COLUMBIA

The Crystal Glass Co., New Westminster.	1907 - 1908
The Midwest Glass Co., New Westminster.	1929 - 1931

MANITOBA

The Manitoba Glass Co., Ltd., Beausejour.	1907 - 1914
The Dominion Glass Co., Ltd., Beausejour.	1913 - 1918

NEW BRUNSWICK

The New Brunswick Crystal Glass Co., East Saint John.	1874 - 1878
The Humphreys Glass Works, Moncton.	1915 - 1920

NOVA SCOTIA

The Nova Scotia (Diamond) Glass Co., Trenton.	1881 - 1892
The Humphreys Glass Works, Trenton.	1890 - 1914
The Lamont (Diamond) Glass Company, Trenton and New Glasgow.	1890 - 1902

ONTARIO

The Mallorytown Glass Works, Mallorytown. First Canadian glass works.	1825 - 1840
The Hamilton Glass Works, Hamilton.	1865 - 1895
The Burlington Glass Works, Burlington.	1875 - 1909
The Napanee Glass Works, Napanee.	1881 - 1883
The Toronto Glass Co., Toronto.	1894 - 1900
The Parkdale Glass Co., Toronto.	1900 - 1913
The Sydenham (Dominion) Glass Co., Wallaceburg.	1895 -
The Erie Glass Co., Port Colborne.	1893 - 1898
The Foster Glass Works, Port Colborne.	1895 - 1899
The Ontario Glass Co., Kingsville.	1899 - 1902
The Jefferson (Dominion) Glass Co., Toronto.	1913 - 1925

QUEBEC

John C. Spence, Montreal.	1845 - 1867
Masson & Company, Como.	1846 - 1847
The Ottawa Glass Works, Como.	c. 1847 - c. 1848
The Canada Glass Works, Como.	1849 - 1875
The Foster Brothers Glass Works, St.Johns.	1855 - 1875
The British-American Glass Co., Hudson.	1855 - 1860
The Montreal Glass Co., Hudson.	1860 - 1865
Above joined Canada Glass Co. in 1865, closed in 1875	
The Canada Glass Co., Hudson.	1865 - 1875

Early Canadian bottle from the Canadiana Department, Royal Ontario Museum.

QUEBEC

The St Lawrence Company, Montreal.	1867 - 1875
The St.Johns Glass Company, St.Johns.	1875 - 1878
The Excelsior Glass Company, St.Johns.	1878 - 1880
The Excelsior Glass Company, Montreal.	1880 - 1883
The North American Glass Co., Montreal.	1883 - 1890
The (early) Dominion Glass Co., Montreal.	1886 - 1898
The Diamond Flint Glass Co., Ltd., Montreal.	1903 - 1913
The Dominion Glass Co., Ltd., Montreal.	1913 -
The Consumers Glass Co., Ltd., Montreal.	1913 -
The Demarais & Robitaille Glass Co., Ltd., Montreal.	1924 - 1925

SEQUENCE OF CHANGES THAT LED TO THE FORMATION OF THE PRESENT DOMINION GLASS WORKS

Foster Brothers Glass Works, St.Johns, P.Q.	1855 - 1875
St.Johns Glass Co., St.Johns.	1875 - 1878
Excelsior Glass Co., St.Johns.	1878 - 1880
Excelsior Glass Co., Montreal.	1880 - 1883
North American Glass Co., Montreal.	1891 - 1902
Diamond Glass Co., Montreal.	1903 - 1913
Dominion Glass Co., Montreal.	1913 -

for further information on these Companies see Page 165.

CANADIAN COMPANIES THAT BECAME PART OF DOMINION GLASS CO — MOSTLY IN THE "DIAMOND GLASS" ERA

The (early) Dominion Glass Co., Montreal.	1886 - 1898
Hamilton Glass Works, Hamilton, Ontario.	1865 - 1895
Toronto Glass Co., Toronto.	1894 - 1900
The Parkdale Glass Co., Toronto.	1900 - 1913
Sydenham Glass Co., Wallaceburg, Ont.	1895 - 1913
Independent Producers Co., Ltd., Toronto.	? - 1912
The Jefferson Glass Co., of Follansbee, W. Va., bought the above company in 1912. The factory joined Dominion in 1913.	1912 - 1925
The Nova Scotia Glass Co., Trenton, N.S. (the above joined Diamond Glass in 1890)	1881 - 1892
The Lamont Glass Co., Trenton, N.S. (joined Diamond in 1898)	1890 - 1902
Dominion Glass Co., Redcliff, Alberta. (this factory still operating)	1913 -
Manitoba Glass Co., Beausejour, Man. Joined Dominion Glass Co., 1914	1907 - 1914 - 1918

Rare amber Beaver fruit jar, collection of Mr and Mrs George Hicks, Listowel, Ontario.

GLASS COMPANIES NOT RELATED TO DOMINION

QUEBEC

Masson & Co., Como, P.Q.	1846 - 1847
Ottawa Glass Works, Como, P.Q.	1847 - 1848
Canada Glass Works, Como, P.Q.	1849 - 1875
John C. Spence, Montreal	1854 - 1867
British-American Glass Co., Hudson, P.Q.	1855 - 1860
Montreal Glass Co., Hudson, P.Q.	1860 - 1865
(joined Canada Glass Co. in 1865, closed in 1875)	
St. Lawrence Glass Co., Montreal	1867 - 1875
Demarais & Robitaille Ltd., Montreal	1924 - 1925
Consumers Glass Co., Montreal later Toronto	1913 - still operating

ONTARIO

Mallorytown Glass Works, Mallorytown, Ont.	
first Canadian company operated.	
from date unknown - closed	1839 - 1840
Burlington Glass Works, Burlington, Ont.	1875 - 1909
Glass Bros. & Co., London, Ontario (potters)	circa 1882 - 1890
Napanee Glass Works, Napanee, Ont.	1881 - 1883
Erie Glass Co., Port Colborne, Ont.	1893 - 1898
Foster Glass Works, Port Colborne, Ont.	1895 - 1899
Ontario Glass Co., Kingsville, Ont.	1899 - 1902

NOVA SCOTIA AND NEW BRUNSWICK

Humphreys Glass Works, Trenton, N.S.	1890 - 1914
Moncton, N.B.	1915 - 1920
The New Brunswick Crystal Glass Co., East St. John, N.B.	1874 - 1878

BRITISH COLUMBIA

Midwest Glass Co., New Westminister, B.C.	1929 - 1931
The Crystal Glass Co., New Westminster, B.C.	1907 - 1908

S.J. Lyman was connected with the St. Lawrence Glass Company, Montreal.

Benjamin Lyman of the above Company was President of The Canada Glass Company, Hudson, P.Q.

SEALERS OR FRUIT JARS — CANADIAN MANUFACTURERS

Excelsior Glass Co., St. Johns	1878 - 1880
Montreal	1880 - 1883
North American Glass Co., Montreal	1883 - 1891
Diamond Glass Co., Montreal	1902 - 1913
The (early) Dominion Glass Co., Montreal	1886 - 1898
Dominion Glass Co., Montreal and elsewhere	1913 - present
Hamilton Glass Works, Hamilton, Ont.	1865 - 1895
Sydenham Glass Co., Wallaceburg, Ont.	1895 - 1913
Burlington Glass Works, Hamilton, Ont.	1875 - 1909
Midwest Glass Co., Winnipeg, Manitoba	1919 - 1931
Ontario Glass Co., Kingsville, Ont.	1899 - 1902
Sager Glass Corp. Ltd., Toronto	
Consumers Glass Co., Montreal and later Toronto	1913 - present
Glass Bros. & Co. (potters), London, Ont. & Brantford, Ont.	1882 -1890

THE ST LAWRENCE GLASS COMPANY

Whilst a great deal is known about the starting of this Canadian factory and the people concerned with it we know very little about the wares that were produced there.

S.J. Lyman, head of a firm of druggists in Montreal, was the 'originator of the company' and as such was toasted at the official opening ceremonies. Enoch Eggington, who had already proved his skills in England and America, was named works manager. William Workman, a merchant/banker and Mayor of Montreal in 1868, raised the capital and provided the initiative to get the Company started and was its first president. Lyman needed supplies of glass-ware and "Druggists' Flint-glass Ware . . Made to Order" was one of the services advertised prominently in the 1868 Products and Manufacturers of the New Dominion.

A. Cochrane, formerly the Montreal agent and secretary of the Canada Glass Company at Hudson, became secretary of the new company. It is interesting to note the president of the Hudson Company was none other than Benjamin Lyman a cousin of S.J. and also head of a drug firm. Others interested in the venture included John Redpath of the sugar refinery and A.M. Delisle, joint owner with William Workman of the ground on which the factory was built. It is reported that the staff at the date of opening was around two hundred persons.

Enoch Eggington was evidently a man of superior ability. He had received his training in England, worked in Germany gaining further knowledge and prior to joining the St Lawrence Glass Company was superintendent of the Portland Glass Company Maine. Unfortunately he died in 1869. Enoch's brother Oliver, who had been with the St Lawrence Company as his assistant, succeeded him as manager. In 1872 Oliver returned to the States and a year later the St Lawrence Glass Comapny finally closed. In 1876 the works was converted to a pottery.

Nova Scotia Glass Company Ltd.,
Trademark c. 1885.

THE NOVA SCOTIA GLASS COMPANY

The Nova Scotia Glass Company was established at Trenton, on the right bank of the East River, in July 1881.

The factory commenced manufacturing glass articles in quantity in September 1881. Skilled men had come from Pennsylvania, Ohio, and Hamilton, Ontario and with local workers formed the staff of the factory. Most of the materials and equipment used was imported from England and America. Coal and lime were the only materials bought locally.

By 1882 the factory was operating 24 hours a day making globes, chimneys for lamps and tablewares. During the next four years the quality of the glass was much improved and more elaborate equipment was imported, and in 1884 it is recorded that over a hundred workers shared a weekly payroll of $1,600.

During the years 1886 and 1887 the quality of the tablewares was of such a high standard and the demand so great that the manufacture of chimneys and globes was curtailed. In 1886 a new design in diamond flint crystal ware, the Victoria Commemorative 1837 - 1887, was made by this factory. During this period other new pressed glass table-wares were made and glassware for the Masonic and Oddfellow Orders.

In 1890 The Diamond Glass Company (now Dominion Glass Co. Ltd) bought the assets of the Company and in 1892 the glassworks was closed.

Advertisement in Lovell's Business & Professional Directory for 1896 — 97.

Bottles on this page from
Nova Scotia glass factories.

Trademark

THE HUMPHREYS GLASS COMPANY

The Humphreys Glass Company of New Glasgow, Nova Scotia, was formed by five brothers. Benjamin, Edgar, Edward, Ephraim and John joined together in 1890 and commenced operations in a factory which had been newly built next to the Nova Scotia Glass Company. John took control since he had been to Pittsburgh, Pennsylvania, to learn the trade.

It is on record that this factory became the leading bottle manufacturers in the Maritimes, with an initial production of some 1,5000 daily. They also produced medicinals, liquor flasks, fruit jars, rolling pins, fly traps and lamps.

The plant was destroyed by fire in 1902, but they quickly built a new and better factory with more modern facilities and separate departments for their various activities. These included one area devoted exclusively to the production of bottles for the Minard's Liniment Co., who ordered in quantities of 300,000 per consignment.

Their customer list included Frasier Thornton & Co., of Cookshire, Quebec, and Saskatoon, Sask., James Roue, Halifax, N.S., Francis Drake, L.H. Packard's Shoe Dressing Mfg., Harvard Bottling Company, Havelock Mineral Spring Co., as well as leading mineral water and soft drink manufacturers, liquor dealers, druggists and other users of bottles in Quebec, New Brunswick and Nova Scotia.

In 1917 the Company moved to Moncton, New Brunswick, in an attempt to combat the fierce competition of the fast growing Dominion Glass Company and rising costs. Production ceased in 1920.

THE LAMONT GLASS COMPANY

Two brothers, Donald and David Lamont, built this factory in 1890 near the Nova Scotia Glass Company site. They were joined in the business by a third brother, Henry.

Products of the factory were globes and lamp chimneys of several kinds, also blown and cut glasswares and clear and coloured bottles.

Competition from larger companies and higher freight rates caused this factory to be sold to the Diamond Glass Company (now Dominion Glass Co.) of Montreal in 1897.

For the next two years, under the new management, production of all kinds of glassware continued. This was brought to an abrupt end when part of the factory was destroyed by fire in 1899.

THE MALLORYTOWN GLASS WORKS c. 1825 — 1840

This glass works is the earliest of the researched glass manufacturers in Canada. Author and historian Gerald Stevens spent a great deal of time and very careful consideration to all the facts before stating "I continue to accept the date of circa 1825". There has been some controversy as to whether this factory was in existence prior to 1839, but our own research leads us to agree with Mr Stevens.

Products of this factory included containers and vessels, all of which were of a pleasing aquamarine blue, due to the fact that oxide of manganese was not included in the materials used. The free-blown method was generally used and excavation of the site produced evidence of bottles, sweetmeat dishes, sugar bowls, tumblers, pitchers, milk bowls and a doorstop type of paperweight.

Mallorytown glass is the most treasured in Canada and very thorough checking should be done before any piece is accepted as authentic. Some examples can be seen at the Sigmund Samuel Canadiana Gallery, Royal Ontario Museum, Toronto.

THE FOSTER BROTHERS GLASS MANUFACTURERS
1855 — 1875.

It is of interest to note that the founders of Foster Brothers were George, Henry and Charles Foster, who moved from America to St John's, Quebec. Some of the workers employed by them were experienced glass blowers from the United States.

The firm is of paramount importance in the history of Canadian glass. First listed as 'The Foster Brothers, Glass Manufacturers', in 1875 they formed a new company — The St John's Glass Company, This company was short lived. In 1878 it was purchased by David and William Yuile, who changed the name to the Excelsior Glass Company.

The company moved to Montreal in 1880 and operated for approximately three years on one site. In 1883 the plant was again moved: this time to the East end of Montreal and again underwent a change of name — The North American Glass Works. This name was used for several years, then the company became the Diamond Glass Company Ltd. In 1902 it was changed to The Diamond Flint Glass Co. Ltd.
It was this company that took over and acquired the control of many of the Canadian glass making firms. These included the following:

The Burlington Glass Company Works, Hamilton, Ontario.
The Hamilton Glass Works, Hamilton, Ontario
The Nova Scotia Glass Company, Trenton, Nova Scotia.
The Lamont Glass Company, Trenton, Nova Scotia.

Later the Diamond Flint Glass Company added other glass companies to the list, both in Ontario and Quebec. The Dominion Glass Company, Montreal (1886-1898), was one of the companies to join the Diamond Flint Glass Company Limited and in 1913 the name was changed again and after amalgamation of all plants directed by 'Diamond Flint' the firm became The Dominion Glass Company Limited and is today the major glass company of Canada.

HAMILTON GLASS WORKS 1865 – 1895

As the Hamilton Glass Works this factory was in continuous operation until 1895 and continues the output of every type of bottle and other containers up to the present date. As the Hamilton Plant of Dominion Glass Co. Ltd. it has the most modern plant on the American Continent and is the most productive in all of Canada.

Fortunately for the collector the products of this factory and the past history of its works and workers have been well preserved. Hamilton is a city with a proud record and has been well served by the "Spectator", established in 1846, which has on micro-film copies of the newspaper back to that time. Residents of the area have always had an interest in the glass works and there are many fine collections of Hamilton glass jars and bottles. The glass produced in this plant was either aquamarine, green or amber.

The Diamond Glass Company, which was formed in 1890 by the merging of several smaller Canadian companies, became the owners of the Hamilton works in 1893. It was in 1906 that the original plant was rebuilt and a new tank constructed to serve the recently imported Owens Automatic Gathering and Blowing Machines. Production was further speeded up by the use of hand operated side lever presses.

When the factory was burned out in 1912 such machinery that could be salvaged was moved to the new plant, which was in the process of being built. The success of the Dominion Glass Company continues and constant improvements have made this works one of Hamilton's leading industries.

Early products included:

Aerated water bottles of the type now known to Canadian collectors as "Pilgrim", several variations of these are shown in the "Evolution of the Pop Bottle" section of this book.

The Hamilton Fruit Jars (several sizes), which had a special type of closure with an iron clamp across the top of the lid secured by an adjustable central screw.

Pickle bottles, sauce bottles, two gallon bottles for water and various other bottles.

Lids for sealers, stoppers, glass targets, globes for lightening conductors and insulators.

Identification is made easy for the collector as Hamilton Works used the entwined "HGC" embossed on many of its products and also embossed "Hamilton Glass Works" in full on many others.

Targets or Bogardus Balls made in Canada can be found with the embossing incised "Made by Rutherford & Co., Hamilton", others with "Gurd & Son, 185 Dundas Street, London, Ontario".

G. Rutherford & Co., Hamilton Glass Works, were listed as bottle manufacturers in 1869, John and William Gurd as "Gurd, John & Son", sewing machine repairers, gunsmiths and rifle makers, Dundas. It is likely that the targets were also made for other Canadian firms.

Finished and unfinished bottles from the site of the Manitoba Glass Works, Beausejour.

Shard of Acme jar found on the site of the Manitoba Glass Works, seen here with complete jar.

All photographs on this page taken from the collection of Mr and Mrs Mac Provick.

THE MANITOBA GLASS COMPANY

by Mac Provick

I couldn't get it out of my mind . . . I just had to see for myself. Having heard bits and pieces concerning a glass factory at Beausejour, and having talked to the son of a man who worked there as a blower wasn't enough; in fact it only whetted my appetite for some personal investigation. I was already firmly "hooked" on glass, especially pressed glass and fruit jars, but I was experiencing a growing curiosity about bottles as well, and a general interest in glass and its manufacture.

My wife and children and I arrived in Beausejour in the morning of May 28th, 1966, to spend what turned out to be a rewarding three days in the area. We discovered that everybody knew about the "old glass factory" on the edge of town, but it was taken for granted, and few, if any people from the outside had taken any interest in it. Mr M.J. Hoban Sr. was our first contact, and he provided much information. Mr Hoban had been keenly interested in the history of the town and district. Other people were interviewed, including a former worker at the plant.

The basic history, as we were able to piece it together, is as follows. In 1905 some of the district's Polish settlers found sand that they judged to be suitable for glass making. A quantity of clay for making the "pots" was imported from Germany. An outdoor, wood fired pot was put into production as an experiment. We were told that the initial production by these Polish workers consisted of bottles of various kinds and sizes, in amber and aquamarine. Whimseys of all sorts were made and given away. We were shown the approximate location of this experimental plant, but no trace of it exists above ground and we found no shards that could be attributed to it.

The second phase of the history of the glass works began in 1906, with the organisation of the Manitoba Glass Company, officially incorporated Jan 23, 1907, under one Joseph Kielbach. Other directors were Edward Kielbach and Gustav Boehm. Workers trained in glass plants in Europe, particularly Poland, were brought out to assist in the erection of the plant and to man it. We heard a number of names of old glass workers and these were Polish for the most part. The guiding light and master craftsman behind the Manitoba Glass Company right from the start was Joseph Wenzoski. He was responsible for the design of the plant as well as the recruitment of skilled labour in Poland. He is said to have had a lot of experience in glass plants in his native land, having overseen the erection of two plants and was connected with the production of sheet glass. His two sons both became skilled blowers, having started out as very young boys. They worked in the plant until it closed.

The foundation for this 1906 building is still to be seen. It was built of wood and some locally made brick was also used. The firebrick for the furnaces was brought in from St Louis, Mo. Principal production was of course containers, particularly bottles in amber and pale green, also some lamp and lantern chimneys. The western market quickly absorbed all the Manitoba Glass production. Winnipeg, only forty miles away, was the gateway to the west and the location of a large number of wholesale and retail establishments, so the largest proportion of the production funnelled through Winnipeg.

In 1909 another change was made, with the building of a much larger plant, allowing two and three shift operations, and the furnaces being fired by gas from coal. The brick and concrete foundation of this later addition are still largely to be seen, although some disturbance was caused in some areas by people salvaging bricks over the years. This time the buildings were of steel frame with wrought iron covering. The main stack is said to have been 120 feet high. I was told that the whole plant, comprising the 1906 and 1907 buildings, employed at peak times from 350 to 400 men and boys. Yearly overhauls and plant alterations took place in July and August during the annual shut-downs. The original Polish and German workers were gradually outnumbered by itinerant workers from Chicago and Terre Haute. One old-timer recalled that the Americans were a particularly high-spirited lot, and they gave the town a sort of "gold rush" flavour,

In the last year of operation an automatic bottle machine was brought into operation, but no one could recall just what was made on it, except that they were generally the smaller types. I found it rewarding to listen to Mr Joe Fogel tell of his experiences. He worked in the plant as a boy of twelve. He vividly described various operations; the furious bustle as containers were being blown and finished; the flocks of visitors on occasion, and the little ceremony performed as the blowers made whimseys and presented them. Mr Fogel said that in spite of the hard work and the terrific heat, these for him were "happy times".

The Manitoba Glass Company plant was never more than a container factory. In its years of flourishing production, from 1908 to 1913, a very large variety of bottles was produced. All this bustling activity in Beausejour was soon to cease however, since in eastern Canada most of the small glass factories had been bought out and closed down by the larger ones. In 1913 the threat of a price war finally caused Manitoba Glass to sell out to the Diamond Flint Glass Company of Montreal. The plant was operated by Diamond Flint for a time, but this concern became part of the Dominion Glass Company, and late in 1913 Dominion Glass ordered the plant closed.

A severe blow was dealt to the area; workers quickly moved to other centres and some took up homesteads. The plant itself stood intact for a time, but eventually all salvageable materials were sold. Bottles and other containers remained in large quantities, many providing targets for young marksmen.

DOMINION GLASS COMPANY -- REDCLIFF WORKS, REDCLIFF, ALTA

THE DOMINION GLASS FACTORY AT REDCLIFF, ALBERTA

This factory was started in February of 1913, producing bottles for the first time in October of that year. Owing to the outbreak of war in Europe the factory closed down in 1914, but re-opened in 1915, at which time an Owens Ten Arm Automatic Machine was installed and three bottle shops went into production.

With the men of the area overseas many of the workers were from the Orient. At the end of the war glass workers returned and with them came experienced men who had been trained in American factories.

Containers, preserving jars, medicine bottles and beer bottles were produced as well as lantern and lamp chimneys. Beer bottles were a major line.

Whimseys from the early days include glass pens, canes, bells, tie racks, animals and cowboy hats.

This factory is still owned and operated by the Dominion Glass Company, Montreal, Quebec.

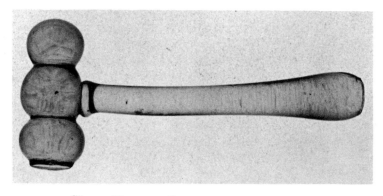

Glass "hammer" made at Beausejour (1906 — 1913) by the late Adolph Opyc of Beausejour.

The three photographs on this page show an interesting assortment of Hamilton area bottles from the collection of Mr and Mrs Harold Jarvis, Grimsby, Ont.

Commemorate Glass Works

On Saturday, November 7, 1970, at 3:00 p.m., an historical plaque commemorating the Burlington Glass Works, one of Canada's most important early glass houses, will be unveiled at the corner of Burlington and MacNab Streets in Hamilton.

This plaque is one of a series being erected throughout the province by the Ontario Department of Public Records and Archives, acting on the advice of the Archaeological and Historic Sites Board.

Saturday's ceremony is being arranged and sponsored by the Head of-the-Lake Historical Society and the Hamilton Museum Committee, whose chairman, Alderman W. W. McCulloch, will act as master of ceremonies. Among those who have been invited to take part are: His Worship V. L. Copps, Mayor of the City of Hamilton; Mrs. Ada Pritchard, M.P.P. (Hamilton West); Mr. Lincoln Alexander, M.P. (Hamilton West); Mr. John Sheeler, a well-known expert on Canadian glass; and Dr. Walter A. Kenyon, Associate Archaeologist, Royal Ontario Museum, who will represent the Province's Historic Sites Board. The plaque will be unveiled by Mr. Gerald Stevens, leading authority on Canadian glass.

The plaque inscription reads as follows:

THE BURLINGTON GLASS WORKS 1874

The Burlington Glass Works, formerly situated here, was one of the most important 19th century glass houses in Canada in terms of the variety and quality of its production. From 1874 to about 1897 skilled artisans produced lamps, tablewares and containers. Glass - production techniques included free-blowing, mould-blowing and pressing in a mould. Pot furnaces produced several different types of glass in a wide range of colours. Glass wares were decorated by cutting, painting, sandblasting, acid-etching and wheelengraving. Archaeological excavations in 1966 and 1969 established the layout of the works and authenticated and enlarged previous knowledge of its output.

The Burlington Glass Works, or as it was known locally, the Flint House, was established in the year 1874 by local Hamilton businessmen and struggled on through strikes by the working men, fires, some of them of disastrous proportions, constant interference in the Company's home market by giant American factories, and by the several changes of ownership which took place during the short period of its operation.

The following list sets out rather graphically changes in the control of the plant:
1) Edward Roberts Kent & Charles and Alfred Myles — 1874-1875.
2) Edward R. Kent & John Neil Tarbox — 1875-1876.
3) John Neil Tarbox — sole owner — 1876-1877.
4) From October 1877 to July of 1878, the property of the Company was held by the old Consolidated Bank of Canada, due to bankruptcy of Mr. Tarbox.
5) Murray A. Kerr & William Godkin Beach — 1878-1881.
6) Murray A. Kerr — either alone, or with partners — 1881-1885.
7) The Hamilton Glass Company Limited — 1885-1891.
8) The Diamond Glass Company (Montreal) — 1891-1897.
9) The factory was evidently closed down about 1897, but the property was held by the Diamond Glass Company and its successor companies. The Diamond Flint Glass Company and Dominion Glass Company Limited until 1927 when the property was acquired by The Corporation of the City of Hamilton and converted into a children's playground.

Some of the best glass-blowers ever employed by any company in this country were on the Company's payroll at one time or another, Mr. William Godkin Beach, who was a partner with Murray A. Kerr during the years 1878-1881, went on to manage The Nova Scotia Glass Company Limited in Trenton, N.S., and after the takeover of that Company in 1892, he became an employee of Diamond Glass Company and its successor company the Diamond Flint Company Limited, and was still employed with them up to the date of his death in 1902. Interestingly enough, the Diamond Glass Company of Montreal had acquired both the Hamilton Glass Company Limited and the Burlington Glass Works in the year previous to their gaining control of the Nova Scotia Glass Company Limited.

Canadian workmen trained at the Burlington Works fanned out across the continent and many other workmen from factories in the United States and Canada and even from as far afield as Europe blew glass at the Old Flint House in Hamilton.

From the beginning, the factory concentrated on the production of lamps and lighting goods and, indeed, had this been the only major field of endeavour, the site would still be well worthy of recognition, however, pressed tableware production was began at the plant between 1885-1890, and to the present-day collector, those items are considered the most important products made at the Works. Many of the decorating techniques of that era were used to advantage at the factory. These included the sandblasting of designs onto lamp globes and chimneys; some cutting of tumblers and stemware (presumably in the late 1870's); the painting and enameling of flower designs on their wares; the manufacture of "art glass" (the combining of two or more colours of glass laid one over the other to obtain a wide variety of colour effects); the etching of glass by the use of acids; and many many other decorative processes.

Most of the pressed table ware designs produced by the company were made also by factories in the United States and possibly in Europe. At this point we are unable to claim any of the products of the factory as being exclusively of their own design, but we can take great pride in the fact that the Company was in the mainstream of North American and European glass technology and that the Canadian market was supplied with glass produced by this Canadian Company, from its beginnings in 1874 to its closing about 1897. Although the factory closed almost three-quarters of a century ago, its products are now being sought by enthusiastic collectors of Canadiana. Canadians of even the most modest means, who are interested in obtaining glass articles which represent tangible links with the past, are able to obtain examples of glass manufactured by Hamilton's Flint House.

Owing to the lack of illustrated catalogues of the Company's production, it has been necessary to determine the factory's output through excavations on the site. In 1966 a dig was undertaken on the site by Dr. Walter Kenyon of the Royal

Section of "Bird's Eye View of the City of Hamilton — 1876"
showing the Burlington Glass Works. No. 63 on map.

Commemorate Glass Works - cont.

Ontario Museum and Mr. Gerald Stevens, author of several works on Canadian glass. During 1967, private excavations were undertaken on the site by Messrs. Behn and Sheeler of Toronto. As a result of the foregoing it was decided that further investigation of the site was warranted and in 1969, thanks to the generosity of Dominion Glass Company Limited, extensive work was done which revealed a much wider production than had been known previously and portions of the foundations of the buildings and furnace were investigated. Miss Helen Sutermeister, the then Curatorial Assistant of the Sigmund Samuel Gallery

Canadian Department of Royal Ontario Museum was in charge of the 'dig' and Miss Janet Holmes, research assistant of the same Department took an active part. Some twenty volunteers gave most generously of their time over the ten-day period that excavations were in progress. The City of Hamilton and the City Parks Department were most co-operative in allowing both the 1966 and the 1969 explorations on the site.

Through the results obtained from the excavations, many of the patterns of pressed tablewares, which had been previously credited to foreign manufacturers, were proven to have

been produced by the Burlington Glass Works and thus the field for collectors of Canadian glass has been further challenged.

When one considers the importance of this factory to the development of the glass industry in this country, and its extensive production, one can well understand the interest which has developed in collecting examples of the tablewares and containers made by this early Canadian glass house.

Mountain City News
Nov. 5, 1970
Courtesy Hamilton Spectator
Hamilton Public Library

THE PLAQUE READS:

THE BURLINGTON GLASS WORKS 1874

The Burlington Glass Works, formerly situated here, was one of the most important 19th century glass houses in Canada in terms of variety and quality of its production. From 1874 to about 1897 skilled artisans produced lamps, tablewares and containers. Glass production techniques included free-blowing, mould-blowing and pressing in a mould. Pot furnaces produced several different types of glass in a wide range of colours. Glasswares were decorated by cutting, painting, sand-blasting, acid-etching and wheel engraving. Archaeological excavations in 1966 and 1969 established the layout of the works and authenticated and enlarged previous knowledge of its output.

Erected by the Archaeological and Historic Sites Board,
Department of Public Records and Archives of Ontario.

C O M M E N T :

The story of the Burlington Glass Works is now well documented and it is evident that Art Glass and high quality wares were produced there. The Burlington Works also made bottles and containers in many weights and sizes.

BEAUTIFUL BLACK

These bottles, dating from the 18th century or earlier, are the beautiful blacks which are most desirable to the collector. To hold such a bottle is to be transported back in Canadian history and one can only guess who first supped from it. Was it the solace of a lonely man or a convivial drink shared with roistering companions? It could have been the bottle a handsome bearded gallant took with him when calling on the lady of his fancy. Was it used to

Eighteenth century bottles, found in Quebec. From the collection of Don Mackenzie.

celebrate a victory or forget a loss? Did a wedding party pass it round and share the contents? It could have been used by a new father to proudly toast a son. It might have been exchanged for furs along with other bottles at a time when "fire water" was as good as gold.

Part of the joy of adding a 'beautiful black' to your own collection is the awareness that no other bottle is exactly like it.

Bottles made prior to the mid-nineteenth century were created in exactly the same primitive fashion as those of the early sixteenth century. As you study the shapes of these bottles you will notice the thick heavy and irregular bases, the push-up on each and every one is different. This is caused by the molten mass of glass seeking a level as it was held downwards in the blowing or when it was lowered into the mold. When the bottle was cooling the bottom distorted still further and had a tendency to balloon or bulge, since this prevented it from standing upright when placed on a flat surface the workers found an easy solution to the problem; with a rod they gave the mass of glass a push-up towards the centre of the bottle. At first this was done with the pontil rod when it was attached to the bottle for finishing; sometimes a slight push was enough, at others a longer thrust was needed. If the worker was fussy, with a good eye, the push-up was likely to be very near the centre, but many were pushed up as one might say unthinkingly and some odd looking hummocks resulted. This phenomena can be observed in the old aqua or green wine and oil bottles making them almost as desirable as the 'blacks'.

Another interesting difference that can be found in the 'blacks' is the presence of streaks or large spots of deep blue-green colour in the area of the push-up. This was caused by the chemical reaction of the iron used in the making of the batch to the gaseous by-products of coal and sulphide fumes which adhered to the rod when it was thrust into the coals to heat up before being used. The resulting colours can be most fascinating.

When the pontil rod was replaced around 1840 any nearby rod was used, sometimes the blow-pipe or other hollow rod, if this happened a little round tip was formed externally at the centre of the push-up.

The neck and lip are other areas where the old bottles vary, since they were reheated for hand finishing they tended to lean a little to the left or right as they cooled, on occasions more than a little.

No blown bottle is twin to its neighbour.

Dark Amber.
Embossed front:
Whiteley's Leith
Scotch Whiskey.
Back:
Whiteley's Leith
re-use of this bottle
prohibited.

Emerald Green.
Marie Brizzard
Pappermint Liqueur.
Height 13½ in.
Embossed:
Bordeaux,
M.B. & Co.

Aqua.
Embossed:
Gordon
Grantown
Scotland
Re-use of bottles
prohibited.

Dark Green.
Embossed:
Hudson Bay
incorporated 1670
also has crest of
Hudson Bay Co.
on base.

An arrangement of bottles taken by the light of the setting sun at Brewery Creek, B.C. The Imperial Quart whiskey bottle, back row left, is 11¾ in. high.

Above — two amber hip flasks with glass stoppers, cork liners.

Left — two old time whiskey bottles from Scotland.

Above — three early 20th century whiskey flasks.

Left — Jim Beam Whiskey - modern.

Canadian whiskeys in Dominion Glass Co. flasks, as shown in their catalogues of the 1895 — 1925 period. Bottle on left "Picnic" shape, others "Shoofly".

The 1899 Hudson Bay Co. catalogue listed only three Canadian whiskey distillers: Gooderham & Worts, offering eleven varieties including a Special 1884, bottled in bond. Seagrams offered '83 Rye and five other types.

Corby's single offering was Corby's IXL.

Left — labelled bottles from early distilleries.

Three early Bols type gin bottles. The stone bottles are becoming hard to find.

"GIN"

The consistently popular spirit originated as a medicine and was prepared first by Franciscus de la Bol in the mid-16th century. He "distilled spirits in the presence of the juniper berry in order to prepare a specific with known diuretic properties".

The French name for Juniper was Genievre which was changed to Genever and Geneva by the Dutch and shortened to Gin by the English.

There are two basic types of gin — that which is produced in Holland and that produced in other countries, mainly England, Canada and America. Holland gin is concocted from rich full bodied spirits and is distilled at very low proof. The other gins are made from highly purified spirits and distilled at very high proof.

In the production of Canadian gin Thomas Molson recorded his efforts to obtain the recipe for making this spirit. He went so far as to advertise in English papers hoping to obtain this information. During visits to the American distilleries he made careful note of what he saw. In August 1836 his firm made their first batch of gin from Rye whiskey and malt. 100 minots of Rye plus 100 minots of barley malt produced 507 gallons of gin, which together with the manufactory expenses cost just over forty two pounds and sold at three shillings and nine pence per gallon, bringing in a total of ninety five pounds.

Later that month a second batch of gin was made from the following ingredients — 534 gals Upper Canada whiskey, 56 lbs Juniper berries, 19 ozs oil of juniper and loaf sugar.

The first recipe used was similar to that of the Dutch, however their product had added

Three sizes of early case gin bottles. Small bottle dark amber, other two black.

"Gin" contd.

juniper and other "botanicals".

Many other flavourings are used by distilleries in England and the U.S.A. and each has its own formulas. Gin is not usually aged, but some American companies do so, thus producing liquor of a pale golden colour.

London Dry Gin is used as a descriptive term and has no geographical significance. The famous "Old Tom Gin" is slightly sweetened. Fruit flavoured gins such as orange, lemon and raspberry are made today.

Sloe gin is not a gin, but a sweet liqueur made from sloe berries.

DRINKS WITH GIN

MARTINIS: Classic Martini — 2oz. Dry Gin, ½oz. Dry Vermouth. Stir with cracked ice, strain into cocktail glass. Serve with olive. Stone Dry Martini — 2¼ oz. Dry Gin, splash Dry Vermouth. Stir and serve as above.

TOM COLLINS: 2 oz. Dry Gin, juice 1 lemon, 1tsp. sugar. Shake well with ice, strain into Tom Collins glass. Fill with carbonated water, decorate with slices of lemon, orange and cherry. Serve with straws.

Rare Prohibition bottle with excise labels,
from the collection of Don Mackenzie.

DATES RELATING TO PROHIBITION

1852   The Honourable Malcolm Campbell, the Postmaster General, introduced a Bill "to restrain the manufacture, sale, and importation of intoxicating liquors".

1853   The Canadian Prohibitory Liquor Law League organised — objective: Total Prohibition.
Brewers and Distillers hire a permanent secretary, who acts as their representative in Toronto, which at that time was the seat of government.

1878   Canadian Temperance Act or "Scott Law" passed. This provided for each locality to exercise an option by plebiscite.

1892   Royal Commission on the Liquor Traffic in Canada appointed.

1895   Report of the Royal Commission tabled.

1901   Prince Edward Island goes "Dry".

1916   Alberta, Manitoba, Nova Scotia and Ontario go "Dry".

1917   Saskatchewan goes "Dry"; also British Columbia, Newfoundland and New Brunswick.

1918   Province of Quebec the only place north of Mexico on the American Continent where total prohibition has not gained the day.

THE TIDE TURNS

The 1921 Liquor Law of the Province of Quebec was the model for most of the liquor legislation which followed in both America and Canada.

1921   British Columbia and the Yukon Territory adopt policy of Government controlled liquor sales.

1923   Manitoba follows suit.

1924   Alberta.

1925   Saskatchewan.

1927   Ontario and New Brunswick.

1928   Nova Scotia.

Canadian "Geneva" gin in Canadian made "case" bottles.

Early Geneva (Dutch) "case" bottles.

BOLS — THE ORIGINAL GIN

The remains of a label on a tall round brown stoneware Bols Gin bottle reads as follows: "Our Firm advantageously known all over the world since its foundation A.D. 1575, has had to suffer from disloyal competition and imitation, and in order to prevent the sale of spurious articles, we hereby give notice that besides "FABRIEK'T LOOTSJE" all our bottles and articles henceforth be accompanied with a label bearing our signature — Lucas Bols and we will in conformity with existing international laws rigoursly prosecute all persons guilty of forging or counterfeiting our Brand".

AMSTERDAM, 1 January, 1868.

The bar, Cook's Tavern, Upper Canada Village, near Morrisburg.

Photograph courtesy of Ontario department of Tourism and Information.

"GOLDEN" OPPORTUNITY

The Molson Story

Molson's Brewery of Montreal started in 1782 and was firmly established by 1786. It was not the first in Canada: the French Apothecary Louis Hebert brewed beer for himself and neighbours. Barley for brewing was planted on Isle d'Orleans by the first Recollet community around 1642. Jean Tallon constructed La Brasserie du Roy in 1671, but closed after only three years of activity.

The first licenced brewer in Montreal was Louis Prud'homme. Some 45 years later in 1690 a brewery was built by Charles le Moyne and was in operation until 1735. In 1704 another brewery was established by a religious and charitable order, the Freres Charon, but it had ceased operations by 1725.

The well-to-do drank mostly wines and spirits. Working men drank spruce beer and sometimes a rather strange beverage called "Chousett", which was made from raw dough fermented in spiced water.

The coming of the British brought a change of taste and soon there were over two hundred licenced beverage houses selling mainly spirits, cheap rum being the most popular. Porter was being imported, but the British soldier welcomed the establishment of the Loides Brewery in 1782. John Molson was a participant in this venture from the beginning and a partner from 1783. He was sole owner by 1784.

It is in 1791 that we find Molsons firmly established with sales of more than 30,000 gallons of ales and beer, including strong, mild, table, small and spruce. Not until around 1800 is any mention made of bottling, previous sales having been made by the hogshead or cask.

Apparently bottles cost three shillings and six pence per dozen, imported in one hundred dozen lots. In 1802 Molson purchased 284 gross of bottles from Goddard & Co. of Quebec. The firm imported bottles of Champagne, Madeira, Port, Sherry, Rum, Brandy, Whiskey and Gin, but strange as it may seem Molsons exported large quantities of Canadian made spirits to England during the period 1820 — 1866.

In Upper Canada Lieutenant-Governor John Graves Simcoe encouraged the setting up of stills, and during the period 1794 — 1801 fifty one licences were issued and doubtless an equal number of unlicenced stills were in operation. There were fewer than 15,000 persons living in the Upper Province at that time.

In Lower Canada James Grant had established a rum distillery in Quebec. Between the years 1767 and 1787 this had a potential of 70,000 gallons, which was then increased to 400,000 by the building of another two distilleries, one of which was in Montreal and was a failure.

Beer bottles intact with labels of yesteryear are highly collectable.

More brewery labels.

By 1820 many other distilleries were established as well as an ever increasing number of breweries.

Molson's first venture in Upper Canada was a brewery and distillery in Kingston, established by Thomas, son of John. The established traders were successfully challenged, goods being offered at Montreal prices. The variety of beers, stout, porter and ale was wide, also produced was an assortment of liquor.

Glass bottles were not used for "Spirits". It was not until 1859 that the pint bottle appeared or that direct retail sales were advertised. It was on August 30th of that year that Thos. & Wm. Molson & Co. advertised their willingness to "supply families and others with their Superior Ales and Porters (in wood or in bottle)". The advertisement included for the first time India Pale Ale (I.P.A.) at one dozen pint bottles for three shillings and three pence.

Figures for 1779 show that three girls worked in the Molson bottling department, Montreal, and that in 1889 the number had risen to twenty nine. The early bottling process was somewhat tedious. The bottles were first unpacked from their nests of straw, then washed, filled and corked by hand. Since the bottles were made of heavy, opaque, dark greenish glass it was impossible to be certain of their complete cleanliness. The straw in which they arrived was a good breeding ground for mice. Sometimes a wee one got trapped in a bottle and was not discovered until some unfortunate drinker was shaken to find a corpse in his glass.

"Draw the curtains close, drink, be sociable and happy".

Of all the claims made by the merchants of the day, none promised anything more delightful than this label extolling the virtues of "English Fettled Porter".
The bottle is broken, but preserved in Bill Hart's collection. Brewer unknown.

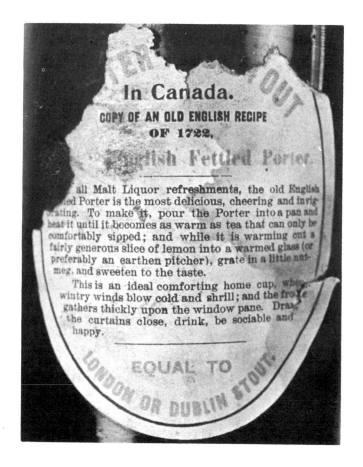

DATES RELATING TO BREWERIES

1808 Miles Williams Sr. founded a brewery in Grants old distillery in Montreal.

1885 The above brewery was acquired by John Aitken, a brewer from Burton-on-Trent, England.

1898 This brewery incorporated as the Union Brewing Co. Ltd.

1899 Canadian Brewing Co. join H.A. Ekers Brewery and become Canadian Breweries Ltd.

1899 Montreal Brewing Co., founded 1840, start to produce Lager beer exclusively.

1909 National Breweries Ltd. was a merger of the following breweries:
Dawes Brewery — Estab. 1811.
William Dow & Co. — Estab. 1808
Ekers Brewery — Estab. 1845.
Canadian Breweries — Estab. 1898.
C.S. Reinhardt.
Douglas & Company.
Beauport Brewery.
George E. Amyot Brewing Co.
Fox Head Brewery.

1891 Crown Cap invented by William Painter of Baltimore and was used by some Canadian firms after 1893, but applied by hand operated presses.

1914 Frontenac Breweries produce light lager beer, which became popular with residents and visitors.

Jan. 1925 Frontenac commence display advertising and announces the addition of "the world's foremost authority on English ale" direct from England.

Feb. 1925 Treasure Hunt announced by large advertisements — "Hundreds of $1.00 and $5.00 cash coupons have been placed under the caps of the bottles".

These advertisements caused a great stir — Molsons declared M. Beaubien, the founder of Frontenac Breweries, to be guilty of unfair trading and countered by cutting prices.

M. Beaubien countered by bringing the prices of Frontenac to the same level. Molson and National cut again. All three groups were losing money and the cut-throat competition did not end until National Breweries Ltd. bought out Frontenac.

Other aspects of the battle included 20 by 60 ft. billboards put up by Frontenac, wooden silhouettes of the famous "Black Horse" of National Brewing adorning the roadsides and barns painted freight car red, vividly decorated with the familiar "La Biere Molson".

So prolific were the advertisements that in 1926 the Brewers Association called on the government to legislate to abolish billboards. The Black Horses were taken down also the massive billboards, but whilst the barns were painted white and Molsons ads disappeared they reappeared with weathering and even today the words can be read on the barns that have survived — La Biere Molson — for in paint, as in everything else, they used only the best.

DATES RELATING TO BREWERIES
(continued from Page 59)

1892 Calgary Brewing and Malting Co. Ltd. formed. "Buffalo Brand" was one of their best known trade marks.

1925 Toronto Brewing & Malting Co. Ltd. formed. In 1928 name was changed to Canada Bud Breweries Ltd. and in 1931 they bought City Club Breweries.

1926 Brewers & Distillers of Vancouver Ltd. were formed by a combination of British Columbia Breweries Ltd. and British Columbia Distillery Co. Ltd.

1926 Silver Spray Ltd. acquired by Calgary Brewing & Malting Co. Ltd.

1928 Associated Breweries of Canada were formed by:
Regina Brewing Co., Regina, Sask.
Prince Albert Breweries, Prince Albert, Sask.
Lethbridge Breweries Ltd., Lethbridge, Alta.
New Edmonton Breweries Limited, Edmonton, Alta.

1930 and 1931 Brewing Corporation of Canada was formed by:
Brading Breweries Ltd., Ottawa, Ont. (Estab. 1863)
British American Brewing Co. Ltd., Windsor, Ont. (Estab. 1882)
Budweiser Brewing Co. of Canada, Belleville, Ont. (Estab. 1925)
Carling Breweries Ltd., London, Ont. & Montreal, Que. (Estab. 1840)
Dominion Brewery Company Ltd., Toronto, Ont. (Estab. 1875)
Empire Brewing Co., Ltd., Brandon, Manitoba. (Estab. 1899)
Grant's Spring Brewery Co., Ltd., Hamilton, Ont. (Estab. 1838)
Kiewel Brewing Co., Ltd., St Boniface, Manitoba. (Estab. 1925)
Kuntz Brewery Ltd., Waterloo, Ont. (Estab. 1840)
Kuntz Beverages Ltd., Toronto, Ont. (Estab. 1930)
Regal Brewing Co., Ltd., Hamilton, Ontario. (Estab. 1875)
Taylor and Bate Ltd., St Catharines, Ontario. (Estab. 1834)

Below — Interesting wood clothes brush advertising bottle from Labatt's Brewery. Collection of Don Mackenzie, Ottawa.

Bottles from Brandon Brewing Company, Manitoba. Both embossed with Beaver Trade Mark.

Two "Canada Bud" beer bottles. The Canada Bud Breweries were great publicists and appealed to the public to drink more beer and provide employment for "countless Ontario workers".

An assortment of labelled and/or embossed beer bottles will provide endless conversation and make an interesting and varied collection.

Left — Three embossed beer bottles. One crown cap type, two with internal threads. Bottles embossed left to right: Ready's Brewery Limited, St John, N.B. James Ready, St John, N.B. (ht. 8¾ in.) James Ready, Brewer, St John, N.B.

Above — Embossed beer bottles. Right: Earlier of two bottles from the Egmondville Brewing Co. Left: Later bottle (amber, 11½ in. tall), embossed — Colbert, Egmondville. The Egmondville Brewery was built by George Weiland and taken over by the Colbert family. It closed in 1913.

Bottom left — Two embossed beer bottles from the Empire Brewing Co. Ltd., Brandon, Manitoba.

Above—Early bottles from the large collection of Don Mackenzie. Centre bottle is an early Labatt beer, treasured and twice repaired.

Left — Two early beer bottles from Manitoba. "Golden Amber Ale" (ht. 11¾ in.) brewed by Edward Drewery, established in 1877.
The "Stout" was one of the Empire Brewing Company brands.
From the extensive collection of Mac Provick.

Quotes from "The Brewers' Agreement" February 14th. 1878.

"The appetite for stimulants is so common, so well nigh universal, that it must be recognized as a desire, a craving, which is natural and which is human".

"A practice so general, commencing in remote antiquity, and common to both savage and civilized people, neccessarily arises from a natural craving in man".

Early Canadian soda water bottles — approx. ¾ size.

Selection of highly collectable "pop" bottles with the distinctive beaver mark.

"POP"

There are several versions given of the origin of soda water and the beginnings of the soft drink industry.

Originally the chemists in Europe were endeavouring to produce something to equal the effervescent waters of the famous mineral springs, because of their therapeutic value. It was Jan Baptista van Helmont (1577-1644) who used the term "gas" when he referred to the carbon dioxide content. Later it was termed "aerated water" by Gabriel Venel who confused the gas with ordinary air. Another experimenter Joseph Black called it "fixed air".

Joseph Priestly was awarded the Copley Medal in 1773 for his "Directions for Impregnating Water with Fixed Air", which was published in 1772. He was of the opinion that there was definite medicinal value in the artificially carbonated water. In 1782 Thomas Henry, an English chemist, described apparatus for producing the waters commercially.

Before long factories and bottling plants were opened right across Europe including London, Dublin, Dresden, Geneva and Paris. By 1807 Benjamin Silliman of Yale College, of Connecticut, U.S.A., was producing bottled "Soda Water". Joseph Hawkins of Philadelphia designed his own machinery and the firm of Shaw and Hawkins was established around 1809. This machinery was actually an improvement of the Schweppes patent process, which had been in operation since 1792.

It was Richard Bewley of England who hit on the idea of adding flavour and in 1768 offered to the public "mephitic julep", which was taken with a draft of lemonade. Soon there were three definite types of beverages: the 'natural' mineral waters, soda waters and flavoured carbonated drinks.

In Ireland the credit for soda water is given to Augustine Thwaites. In the history of Cantrell and Cochrane, famous Dublin soft drink firm there is this statement:

"Soda water was invented by Augustine Thwaites who had an apothecary shop in Dublin. In 1769 he discovered that he could produce an effervescent water containing soda.

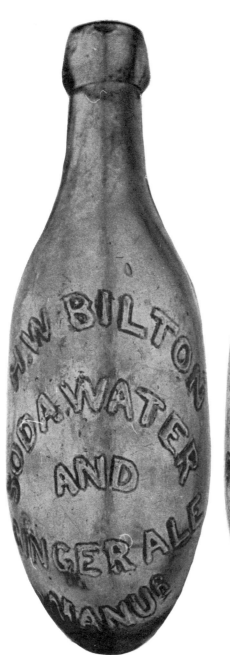

Early H.W. Bilton bottle, embossed on both sides. Collection of Mary Sherb of Hamilton, Ontario.

Very rare Glendenning "torpedo" bottle, salvaged from off the North Arm, Halifax, N.S. Stephen Giza collection.

Early Pilgrim bottle dug at Brandon, Manitoba, by Douglas Smith of the Parkland Bottle Club.

Drawing courtesy of Parkland Bottle Club, Saskatchewan.

W. Pipe bottles are found in various shapes, colours and sizes and with different embossings. Above — left to right: W.Pipe, Kingston & W.Pipe, Kingston, C.W. Others seen embossed W. Pipe, Ottawa

MEDICAL HALL

The Medical Hall was established by Kenneth Campbell in Montreal during 1856. This firm of manufacturing wholesale druggists were in business over a very long period as advertisements placed by American drug manufacturers in the Canadian Lancet during the 1890's list them as their Canadian agents.

Many of the compounds made by Campbells were internationally known and various shapes and sizes of bottles embossed or labelled with their name are found from coast to coast, mainly in clear and aqua. It is likely that all the bottles were made in Canada — first in the St Johns Glass Works and the Como Hudson Works & later in the Diamond Flint Co. Works.

A Medical Hall was established by T. Bickle & Sons in 1835 in the town of Hamilton, Ont, but whether there was any connection between the two firms is still to be established. T. Bickle & Son were steady advertisers in the Hamilton Spectator Almanacs of the 1870's.

Together with his son he formed a partnership and they produced Single and Double Soda Waters. The bottles which they used were rounded and pointed. The corks were wired in place to keep them moist and to prevent them from coming out since the gas pressure was such that the corks would pop out unless secured. The firm was later taken over by Cantrell and Cochrane and later Cochrane's name only appeared on the bottles".

In Australia the credit is given to Nicholas Paul, a Swiss, who invented "a glass bottle of an oval shape with stout walls" in 1790. This bottle was termed a "drunken bottle", since it was not possible to stand it up.

In England in 1814 a Mr Hamilton designed 'torpedo' bottles for J. Schweppe & Co.

Wm. H. Glendenning of Dartmouth was the first manufacturer of soft drinks in Nova Scotia, possibly just prior to 1836.

R.A. Pilgrim of Hamilton was producing these drinks in Ontario in 1848.

Alex Phillips of the Pioneer Soda Water Works of Victoria B.C., was the first in Western Canada, circa 1858.

Right across Canada, as in America, Europe and Australia the soft drink industry spread and every town of any size had a manufacturer of a social beverage, which had started in the sixteenth century as a likely medicine.

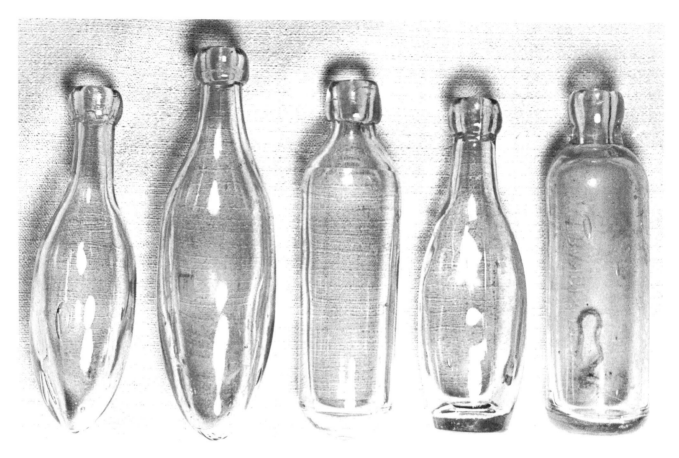

Bottles from the collection of Mr and Mrs Dan MacDonald, Moncton, N.B.

EVOLUTION OF THE "POP" BOTTLE

The first pop container was most likely the torpedo shaped bottle, which dates back to 1769 and was used later by Cantrell and Cochrane of Belfast and Dublin. The pointed base was replaced by a rounded one: this bottle also was made so that it would not stand. Both bottle styles were used in Ireland, England, Canada and America.

The Americans designed a shorter version of the bottle levelling off the base. The first of these was made around 1840, examples having been found with particles of metal embedded in the pontil mark.

With the improvement of closures there was no need to keep the bottles lying down, so the next type was the flattened round. In 1873 the Codd Patent Stopper gave us another type. The Canadian Patent for a variation of the Codd was registered in 1876. Special machinery was required for the filling of these bottles, which had to be held upside down to

allow the liquid to enter. Only one firm in Nova Scotia is known to have used them — The Milton Aerated Water Works, Queens Co. The system, with its expensive bottles, proved uneconomical. The "empties" frequently did not return to the bottling plant, since children broke the bottle to get the precious marble. The embossing on bottles indicates that several Ontario firms used the Codd Stopper.

Bottles with internally threaded necks were made to take a screw type stopper with a rubber ring and were imported from Britain. Some of the stoppers with threads were made of wood. This was in 1902, but these were not popular and few were used after 1903.

In 1879 the Hutchinson Closure was invented and the bottle neck was shortened to better contain the small rubber disc.

The "Crown Cap", still in use today, was patented in 1891, but not generally accepted

Right —
Crown Caps
were used
on stone and
glass bottles.

until the automatic machine became part of the bottle makers equipment. By 1920 all other types of closure went out of use and the bottle itself had by then become much lighter in weight, uniform in texture and standardized in colours. Different soft drink manufacturers had bottles specially designed and many variations can be collected.

The majority of stone ginger beer bottles were imported from England, often being used as ballast on returning ships. By the mid-1870's potteries in Canada were making bottles to order for various firms. They also made large pottery jugs, many of which were labelled under glaze.

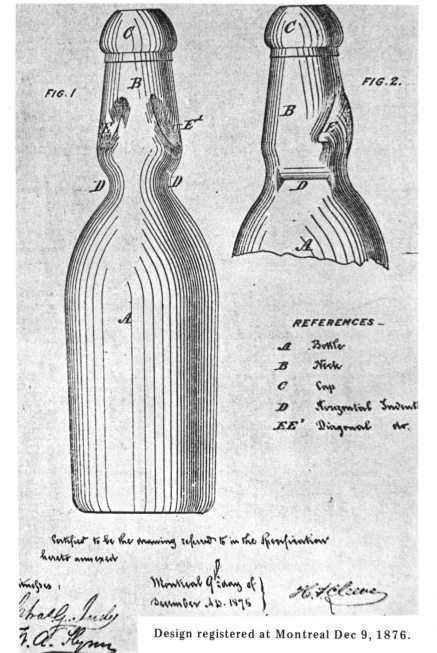

Design registered at Montreal Dec 9, 1876.

A Milton Aerated Water Works bottle with Codd stopper. Note difference in design of lip from that in Canadian Patent drawing.

THE "PILGRIM" STORY

The manufacturing of soda and mineral waters was started in Hamilton, Ontario by Robert A. Pilgrim around 1848.

The first bottles used were crude, heavy, blob topped and some were torpedo-shaped whilst others had rounded bases. No two were exactly alike. These bottles have been found in different colours and include a deep, attractive cobalt blue. The known Pilgrim bottles are embossed R.A Pilgrim and with the Trade Mark—an eagle with outspread wings balanced on a rock. This trade mark was used continuously until 1920, with name changes from R.A. Pilgrim to R.A. Pilgrim & Co. to Pilgrim Bros. to Pilgrim Bros & Co to Cummer & Son.

Where the first bottles were made has not been ascertained. There was a Canadian factory in Como, Quebec at that time also bottles were imported into the country from both Europe and America. After 1865 it was possible to obtain the bottles locally for in that year the Hamilton Glass Company was started.

R.A. Pilgrim was listed as a brewer in 1856 but whether beer bottles with his trade mark

exist has not been recorded. He was listed as a maker of ginger wine in 1858 and four years later he joined Wm. Bone and Wm. J. Clark and formed R.A. Pilgrim & Co. Soda water, Seltzers, and Ginger Wine were produced by the company. This venture could not have been successful, as in 1867 he is again trading as R.A. Pilgrim making soda water and dealing in groceries and liquors. The grocery business occupied his activities until 1870, but in that year he ventured on another partnership, this time with a Mr Vandewater and the directory shows Robert A. Pilgrim & Co. This lasted until 1877, when he again reverts to R.A.Pilgrim soda water manufacturer, and is so listed until 1882.

For a period of one year Mr Vandewater continued to make soda water at the factory and possibly bottles could be found for the 1876 period with Vandewater embossed.

Over the years the sons of Robert had learned the business and took over the firm as Pilgrim Bros when their father died in 1883. The brothers Edward, Frederick, Robert and Sydney carried on the soft drink manufacturing together until 1901 — 02.

In 1903 the firm became Pilgrim Bros & Co, comprising John H. and A.J. Cummer and Edward Pilgrim. It would seem that the other brothers had decided to start up business elsewhere.

A third generation Pilgrim commenced his own factory as a mineral water manufacturer in Hamilton and is shown in the directory as T.M. Pilgrim & Co.

In late 1903 the original Pilgrim firm became Cummer & Son. Both T.M. Pilgrim & Co as well as Cummer & Son are shown in the Hamilton directories until the year 1910. The Cummer & Son firm became the Hamilton Mineral Water Company in 1910, but reverted to Cummer & Son in 1914. The father and son business continued until 1920 when it was acquired by Sutherlands.

Sutherland's bottles are embossed variously with Sutherland—Hamilton, Sutherlands Ltd., Sutherland's Beverages Ltd., and Sutherland's Ginger Ale Ltd. (The authors have found some Sutherland bottles in cornflower blue glass)

For further information on Sutherlands see Page 227.

LABEL COLLECTION

COLLECTION OF CARBONATED BEVERAGE (SOFT DRINK) -
PAPER LABELS FROM THE PILGRIM MINERAL WATER CO.
PLYMOUTH SPRINGS - AYLMER, P.Q. - MAY, 1964.

BOTTLE-
GLASS
DUMP,
Aylmer, P.Q.

THE - METHOD OF RESTORATION - D.C. MacKenzie.

The labels were originally found in closely matted "lumps"
or "chunks among the bottle glass debris.

(1) "Lumps" placed in a large glass specimen jar of water &
soaked for 2 to 3 weeks.

(2) Then each "lump" taken out of the jar, separately, - placed
in a further bowl of water and the labels seperated pains-
takingly from each other with a flat table knife and wooden
pointed stick. Much time and patience required to remove
each label from its neighbour, as some of the glue still
remains and they tear very easily in this water-soaked
condition.

(3) Individual labels then placed on a large sheet of brown
kraft paper from which they easily "come away" after
approx. 8 hours natural drying process.

(4) Labels then pasted with rubber paper cement to loose-
leaf pages and then assemebled in alphabetical and
chronological order.

The "label lumps" were excavated from within the heart of
the glass deposit.

Pilgrim Story contd.

When the brothers broke up the Pilgrim
Bros. combine, F.M. started the F.M. Pilgrim
firm in Brockville and Aylmer, Quebec.

A.T. Pilgrim had a manufactury in Brantford
Ontario and it is likely that other Pilgrim
embossings or labels are to be found.

Collectors interested in the Pilgrim series
could add to the information given here by
consulting local directories and libraries.

The very elaborate embossing on the bottle above reads:

ST LEON MINERAL WATER CO. LTD.

TRADE MARK   REGISTERED

HEAD OFFICE   TORONTO

CANADA

Two J. Tune & Son bottles.

In the County of Middlesex directory for 1889 there appears the following:

JAMES TUNE & SON

"A marked and important industry in the city of London is the manufacture of carbonated beverages, and among the most actively engaged in this branch of commercial trade is the firm of James Tune & Son, proprietors of the London Soda Water Works. The manufactory which these gentlemen conduct is well equipped with the most modern and improved machinery, and their product is unsurpassed by any similar manufactory in the Dominion, and embraces the following list of goods: Ginger ale, champagne, crab apple cider, phosphated champagne sherbert, double soda, lemon soda, sasparilla, Georgia mineral water, seltzer water in siphons and St Leon mineral waters. The business of this firm was first established at Simcoe in 1880, and in 1883 removed to London; since which time Mr Tune has been recognized as one of London's enterprising and successful business men. Their success has been largely due to their enterprise and energy, as well as to the superior nature of their product, in which both skill and experience have been combined in making equal to the most noted manufacturers of the Old Country. The firm give their personal attention to their business, even to the most trivial details, and have built up an enviable name for the honourable methods of conducting their business, and the uniformly gentlemanly treatment of those with whom they have business intercourse. James Tune, the senior partner and founder of the business, is a native Canadian, and he was born in Brantford, County of Brant, March 30, 1837. His parents, Robert and Elizabeth (Dean) Tune, were both of English birth. When the father first came to Canada he settled in Little York, now Toronto. The subject of this sketch was reared in Canada at the confectionery business, and following this calling for 15 years. He was married in 1862 to Miss Sarah Hambidge, a native of Canada, to whom were born four sons; Charles Henry, George Edward, William Alfred and John Albert. Charles Henry, the eldest son, is associated with his father in the business".

The last entry in the London records that could be found showed an Alfred Tune Ltd., 104 Dundas St., manufacturers of carbonated beverages. This was dated 1932, thus it would seem that Tune's had been a continuing business from 1880 until a date later than 1932.

COCA COLA BOTTLES

The first bottles used by the Coca Cola Company, when they started around 1890, were of the blob top type with the Hutchinson closure.

There are many shapes and sizes to be found in the Coca Cola bottles made prior to 1917 when they standardized the shape and started to use what collectors term the "Mae West".

The glass used was usually clear or green, but special batches were made in orange carnival, blue and a very rare flashed gold.

Green Coca Cola bottle.

Three pre-1917 Coke bottles.

Nova Scotia & New Brunswick mineral water bottles.
Left to right: Francis Drake, New Glasgow, N.S.,
King Bottling Co., N.S., R.J. Garnett, St John, N.B.

Three bottles — Felix J. Quinn
Halifax, Nova Scotia, 1888 - 1914.

Francis Drake contd.

A large trade is done by this house,
the invigorating and refreshing, non-
intoxicating drinks, at the same time
exhilarating and revivifying. The
capacity of the works is one thous-
and dozen per week and their goods
are always in active demand. The
members of the firm are Messrs.
Francis, Newton and Sarah Drake,
all of whom are natives of Halifax,
but who have lived in New Glasgow
for the last twenty years".

Above — left to right:
Aqua bottle, embossed Essex Centre, Hutchinson stopper.
J.M. McKenzie, Sydney, C.B.
Amherst Mineral Water Co. Taylor & Tennant, Props., Amherst
Aqua bottle, Shediac Beverage Co., cross trade mark.   N.S.

Left — bottles of the Sussex Mineral Springs Co., Sussex, N.B. This Company started in 1885 — various bottles & embossings were used.

Left to right:
Sussex Mineral Springs Ltd., Sussex, N.B. (earliest bottle)
Sussex Beverage Company, Registered (height 10¾ in)
Stone bottle — inscription can be read.
Sussex Mineral Springs.

Lower left picture:
Three more "Sussex" bottles
Note stone bottle in centre:
Sussex Ginger Ale Ltd.

FRANCIS DRAKE OF NOVA SCOTIA

Francis Drake of New Glasgow, Nova Scotia, is believed to have been in business from 1867 — 1925.

With his father-in-law, William Glendenning of Dartmouth, he started the firm which was to become one of the best known in the Province of Nova Scotia.

In "Our Dominion" published in 1887 by The Historical Publishing Co. of Canada, the following appears:

"The tendency of the present age is undoubtedly in favour of temperance drinks, and the manufacture of these refreshing and non-intoxicating beverages is an important feature of our industrial pursuits. An old established and prominent house devoted to this line of business in New Glasgow is that of Mr Francis Drake, whose firm is engaged in the manufacture of carbonated beverages, nerve food and fruit syrups. This establishment dates its inception back to some twenty years ago, having been founded in 1867, since then their productions have won their way to popularity with wonderful rapidity. The premises occupied consist of a two storey building, 20 x 70 feet in dimensions, equipped with every modern machinery and operated by steam. The products of the factory consist of lemon, strawberry, raspberry, orange, pineapple, vanilla, and other syrups; also banner ginger ale, in quarts and half pints, specially prepared for hotels and family use; Belfast ginger ale in half pints and siphons, also lemonade, sarsaparilla, champagne cider, soda water etc. An excellent preparation here manufactured is the Standard Nerve Food, which is highly endorsed by the medical faculty.

Four siphons above, left to right:
Pure Springs Co., Ottawa, Ontario.
W.E. Rummings, Nanaimo, B.C.

Sutherlands Ltd., Manufacturing
Chemists, Hamilton, Ontario.
The Maple Leaf Aerated Water Co.,
Hawkesbury, Ontario.

French siphon, Ht. 12 in. made for
William Givan, Moncton, N.B.
Blob top bottle embossed William
Givan, Moncton, N.B. and on reverse
side Aerated Water.

THE SODA SIPHON

The siphon for carbonated beverages was first
known in the form of the "Regency Portable
Fountain", patented in 1825 by Charles Plinth.
This fountain utilized a stop-cock, the modern
siphon has a spring valve.

In 1837 Antoine Perpinga patented the
"vase siphoide". This was essentially the siphon
as we know it today. A great many siphons
were manufactured in France and required a
filling device.

Hotels and bar rooms always had the siphon
handy. There are a few variations in style to
be found, the hour-glass wire covered type is
one of the earlier models and probably the
hardest to find.

The siphon is quite decorative and made in
many different colours. Since most are acid
etched with the names of the users very
interesting collections can be made.

Hutchinson's Patented Siphon Filler

1.	Body Cover (Cage)	$1.25	7. Stand	$5.00
2.	Body (Cage)	1.25	8. Treadle	1.25
3.	Body Base	2.00	9. Connecting Link	.50
4.	Valve Lifter with Roller	.75	10. Connecting Rod with	
5.	Connecting Fork	1.75	Coupling and Spring	1.50
6.	C. I. Seat	.75	11. Rod Coupling	

This machine is especially constructed with the very best material throughout. It is so arranged that you can fill all sized siphon bottles. Guaranteed to give satisfaction.

Price, complete with Filling Head $23.00

Absolutely Pure Ginger—XXX Brand

From the W.H. Hutchinson & Son Catalogue of Bottlers Machinery and Supplies for 1912.
Courtesy Don Mackenzie

Photograph taken at Morris Antiques, Quebec City.

Highly desirable hour glass siphon.

W·H
HUTCHINSON
&SON
CHICAGO

HEADQUARTERS
FOR
SODA WATER FLAVORS
BOTTLERS' MACHINERY
AND SUPPLIES

1912

THE BEST STOPPER FOR CARBONATED DRINKS

THE refreshing, sparkling quality of carbonated bottled beverages depends primarily upon their being charged heavily with carbonic acid gas, and upon the bottles being stoppered and closed hermetically so as to prevent any escape of gas; otherwise the drinks are flat and insipid, losing their sharp, pungent "snap" which is their principal charm.

The Hutchinson spring stopper is specially designed and adapted to the purpose, and is by far the most effective and satisfactory stopper for bottled carbonated drinks. Unlike other stoppers, the greater the pressure within the bottle, the tighter and more effective the closure, the gas pressure acting behind and against the valve. It is obvious that when bottles are closed with ordinary corks, or with any exterior method of closure, the gas pressure within the bottle operates to blow out the cork or to blow off the valve, and more or less leakage is constantly going on.

Another point of superiority of the Hutchinson stopper is the fact that in filling the bottles all the atmospheric air is eliminated from the bottle, as in closing the bottle the stopper is drawn up by the bottling hook, and nothing is forced down upon or into the bottle, as is the case with other methods of closure.

When the Hutchinson stopper is used, no implement of any kind is necessary to open the bottles, the stopper being simply pressed down with the hand, making it the most convenient in opening.

Hutchinson Bottling Table

Table complete with Bottling Attachment........$25 00
Syrup Gauge Extra.

The Table top is 2-inch oak, well seasoned and closely joined, polished and oiled. The uprights are steel, sliding in 6-inch guides, which are cast in one piece with the bed plate. In the center of the bed plate is a cup projecting down through the table. In filling a half-pint bottle it rests on the cover of this cup. By removing the cover, a pint or quart bottle may be filled without further changes.

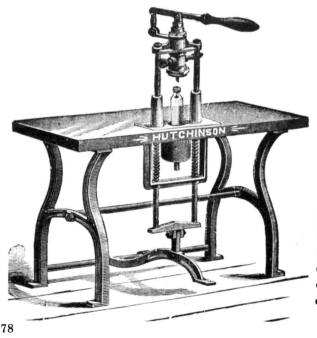

TRADESMEN AND MERCHANTS WITH BUSINESSES RELATED TO BOTTLES

from Lovell's Business and Professional Directory for 1896 — 97

Brewers and Maltsters.

Simcoe Steam Brewery.. Harris, O.
Roy J. A ....Belleville, O.
Severn William .... "
Kuntz L............ Berlin, O.
Bixel Brewing and Malting
  Co., Ltd..........Brantford, O.
Bowie & Co......Brockville, O.
Morris J. & T., Queen..
          Charlottetown
Cauchon — ..Chateau Richer, Q.
Schumacher Bros ..Chesley, O.
MacPherson, Gordon & Co...
          Cobourg, O.
Maritime Brewing and Malt-
  ing Co......Dartmouth, N.S.
Davies Robt..........Doncaster, O.
Schwartz Jno. S......Formosa, O.
Holliday Thomas ...Guelph, O.
Sleeman George ....
Dawes & Co., 209 Barrington.
          Halifax
Keith A., & Son, 88 Lower
  Water .... "
Lager Beer brewery .... "
Ol and J. C., 41 Bedford row "
Gompf John, cor John and
  Burlington....... ....Hamilton
Grant - Lottridge Brewing
  Co., Ltd., 167 Bay N ...... "
Kuntz Henry, 19 Bay N ...... "
Ontario brewery, John Bur-
  lington .... "
Brasserie de Joliette Joliette, Q.
Imperial Brewery Co., Ltd..
         Kamloops, B.C.
Bajus' brewery, 308 Welling-
  ton....................Kingston
Dawes & Co. See adv. Lachine, Q.
Lindsay brewery.... Lindsay, O.
Carling Brewing and Malting
  Co., cor Talbot and Ann.London
Hamilton Jos., 197 Ann ...... "
Labatt Jno., foot Talbot ...... "
Canadian Brewing Co...Montreal
Dawes & Co., Lachine,
  P.Q., office 521 St James. .
  See adv p. 636 .... "
Dow Wm., & Co., 36 Chaboil-
  lez sq .... "
Ekers' brewery, 409 St Law-
  rence .... "
Labatt J., 123 Delorimier av "
Molson John H. R., & Bros.,
  1006 Notre Dame .... "
Montreal Brewing Co.,
  133½ Notre Dame .... "
Reinhardt G., & Sons, 529 Av
  de l'Hotel de Ville .... "
Silver Creek Brewing Co., of
  Guelph, Ont., 8 Lemoine .. "
Slemans Brewery of Guelph, ·
  Hasenfratz August, & Co....
         Nanaimo, B.C.
Union Brewing Co., Ltd.... "
Weigel Peter .... "
Reisterer Robt. N....Nelson, B.C.
Huether Henry......Neustadt, O.
Andrezjewski John.......
      New Westminster, B.C.
Jamieson C. M. .... "
Anderson Arthur, 726 Wel-
  lington.................Ottawa
Brading H. F., 457 Welling-
  ton .... '
Ottawa Brewing and Malting
  Co., Ltd., 851 Wellington "

Eaton Bros...... Owen Sound, O.
Schwan Bros. .... "
Sleemans Brewery Agency,
  Geo. Wilkinson .... "
Crystal Spring brewery..Perth, O.
Calcutt Henry.. Peterborough, O.
Cronmiller & White........
      Port Colborne, O.
Ambrose Winslow Brew-
  ing and Malting Co., Ltd.
  See adv p. 921.... Port Hope, O.
Fisher Bros.......Portsmouth, O.
McCarthy John, & Sons, Ltd.
      Prescott, O.
Prescott Brewing and Malt-
  ing Co., Ltd. .... "
Bernhardt Peter......Preston, O.
Hummel David .... "
Beauport Brewing Co., 44½ St
  Joseph........ ...... Quebec
Boswell & Bro. .... "
Proteau & Carignan, 263 St
  St Paul .... "
Rock Spring brewery, Sau-
  vageau & Arago .... "
Allen O. H ...Revelstoke, B.C.
Righton Thomas .... "
Rossland Spring brewery..
      Rossland, B.C.
Heuser H..........Sarnia, O.
Odell C. J. & F. W..Sherbrooke, O.
Taylor & Bate..St Catharines, O.
Garnett Robert J., 124 Brus-
  sels ....St John
Jones S., 200 Carmarthen "
Ready J. A., 97 Union ...... "
Clouthier Damase.........
  Ste Therese de Blainville, Q.
Rudolph & Begg....St Thomas, O.
Devlin & Steele......Stratford, O.
Empire brewery .... "
Strathroy Brewing and Malt-
  ing Co...........Strathroy, O.
Luke J., & Sons.. Tilsonburg, O.
Copland Brewing Co., 55 Par-
  liament.... ....Toronto
Cosgrave Brewing Co., Ltd.,
  The, 295 Niagara .... "
Davies Brewing and Malting
  Co., N S Queen E junction
  King E .... "
Dominion Brewery Co., Ltd.,
  470 Queen E .... "
Eaton Bros., 4 Louisa ...... "
Korman Mrs. M. E., 105
  Duchess .... "
O'Keefe Brewery Co., Ltd.,
  11 Gould .... "
Ontario Brewing and Malt-
  ing Co., 311 King E ...... "
Reinhardt & Co., 2 Mark .. "
Silver Creek brewery, 23
  Church .... "
Toronto Brewing and Malt-
  ing Co., Ltd, 274 Simcoe "
Baker & Williams, Pendu...
      Vancouver, B.C.
Columbia Brewery, Kappler
  & Co., Powell .... "
Doering & Marstrand, 7th av "
Excelsior Brewing Co., Ltd.,
  Esquimalt road...Victoria, B.C.
Farrall H., jun., Esquimalt rd "
Leahy John, 124 Johnson "
Victoria Phenix Brewing Co.,
  Ltd., 191 Government "
Farquharson & Grainger....
      Walkerton, O.
Walkerville Brewing Co....
      Walkerville, O.

Mineral Waters.

Grenfell Mineral Water Fac-
  tory..........Grenfell, N.W.T.
Donovan W. H., 41 Gran-
  ville ....Halifax
Pilgrim Bros. & Co., 12
  Jarvis.............Hamilton
Christin Joseph, & Cie., 149
  Sanguinet ....Montreal
Cormond F., & Co., 17 Rou-
  ville .... "
Domphousse J., 35 Rivard "
Harte J. A , 1780 Notre Dame "
Radnor Water Co., Canada
  Life bldg, 189 St James "
Robillard C., & Co., 209 St
  Andre .... "
St Leon Water Co., 54 Vic-
  toria sq .... "
Borthwick Wm., 120 Rideau. "
      Ottawa
Grand Hotel Co., 74 Sparks "
Huckels A., & Co., 326 Queen "
Peterboro Mineral Water
  Co.............Peterborough, O.
Havelock Mineral Spring
  Co ....Petitcodiac, N.B.
Preston Mineral Springs ...
      Preston, O.
Mineral Water Co...........
      St Hyacinthe, Q.
Hawthorn Mineral Springs..
      Thornhill, O.
Langstaff John .... "
Boyle & Libby, 349 Dundas.
      Toronto
Clark Bros., 30 William "
Fletcher Manfg Co., The, 440
  Yonge .... "
Forrest Lorenzo, 311 Yonge "
Guggisberg & Co., 103 Ade-
  laide W .... "

Matthews James, 29 Ossing-
  ton av..................Toronto
O'Connor Thos., 126 George "
Robertson Wm., 106 Nassau "
St Leon Mineral Water Co.,
  The, Ltd., 101½ King W "
Verner Wm. A., 16 Spruce "
Walsh James, 122 Berkeley "
Wilson Chs., 517 Sherbourne "
Fairall Henry S., Esquimalt
  rd..................Victoria
Barton Albert......Walkerton, O.

Pottery and Stoneware.

Hart Bros. & Lazier. See
  adv p 16.......... Belleville, O.
Saunders Cabel.......Bolton, O.
The Brantford Stoneware
  Mf'g Co., Ltd., J. P. Hemp-
  hill, secretary-treasurer..
      Brantford, O.
Schuler W. B. .... "
Bierenshiel A......Bridgeport, O.
Cornhill James......Chatham, O.
Eby William ......Conestogo, O.
Flack & Van Arsdale.......
      Cornwall, O.
Burns Samuel R....Doncaster, O.
Campbell R., 96-118 Locke S
      Hamilton
Cranston J., & Son, 210
  Garth. See adv .... "
Foster S. P., & Co., Main,
  west of Garth. See adv p 458 " .
Hamilton Pottery, R. Camp-
  bell, 96-118 Locke S "
Wentworth Pottery, 210
  Garth .... "
Fitzmaurice B. A.,Adelaide,
  near Grey..........London, O.
Star Pottery, John Pegler,
  prop, 95 Rectory "
Joyce Thomas A............
      Lower Stewiacke, N.S.
Davey W. J......Owen Sound, O.
Elliott Adam......Russell, O.
Caledonian Pottery of St
  Johns.............St Johns, Q.
Dominion Sanitary Pottery
  Co. .... "

Soda Water Manufacturers.

Horton & McGregor.. .. ..Chatham, O.
Lambert & Turner .... "
Quinn F. J., 371 Barrington.. ..Halifax
Roue J., Wood's wharf, 121 Lower
  Water .... "
Walker E., 77 Brunswick ...... "
Whelan & Ferguson, 244 Barrington "
Williams H. A.. .. ..Huntsville, O.
Seeley C. H. ......Kemptville, O.
Reids George.. .. ..Markham, O.
Givan's William Sons ....Moncton, N.B.
Allan Robert, 620 Dorchester..Montreal
Brossaille Moise, 718 St Andre "
Christin Jos., & Cie., 149 Sanguinet "
Cooper Arthur, 79 Papineau av "
Ferland A., & Co., 151 St Andre "
Gurd Chas., & Co., 43 and 45 Jurors "
Lafreniere Jos., 1020 Ontario "
Milloy P., 121 St Andre "
Robillard C., & Co., 209 St Andre "
Roman Joseph, 31 1-2 St Urbain "
Rowe Frank W., & Co., 639 La-
  gauchetiere .... "
Lawrence Lewis..... .. .. ..Nanaimo, B.C.
Howard George, 201 Besserer.. ..Ottawa
Laughingbon H........ ..Parry Sound, O.
Belch E., & Co.. .. ..Picton, O.
Paquet & Fluet, 63 des Prairies..Quebec
Cordeau & Lajoie.. .. ..St Hyacinthe, Q.
Hutchinson T. H.. .. .. ..St Thomas, O.
Stratford Soda Water works, A.
  H. King, prop.. .. .. ..Stratford, O.
Taylor R.. .. ..Strathroy, O.

Verner John, 100 Berkeley.. .. ..Toronto
Verner Wm. A., 16 Spruce "
Wilson Chas., 517 Sherbourne "
Darlington Charles.. .. .. ..Uxbridge, O.
Monette Victor.. .. .. ..Valleyfield, Q.
Calley & Co., Ltd.. .. ..Vancouver
Morley Christopher, 7 Waddington
  Alley .. ..Victoria, B.C.
Phillips Bros, 8 Yates "
Thorpe & Co., Ltd, Gorge road "
Blackwood Bros.. .. ..Winnipeg

*Soda Water Apparatus.

Collins H. A. Co., The, 126 Bay. See adv
p 1158............................ .....Toronto

*Soda Water Fountains.

Fletcher Manufacturing Co., The,
  440 Yonge.. .. ..Toronto

Five pottery ginger beer bottles from New Brunswick and Nova Scotia.

STONE GINGERS

Ginger beer came into use around 1809. A recipe for home brewed ginger beer required:

Bruised Jamaica Ginger . . . . 6 parts.
Cloves . . . . 3 parts.
Hops . . . . 3 parts.
Liquorice Extract . . . . 2 parts.
Gentian . . . . ¼ part.

To 200 parts water add 5 parts of the above mixture, boil for 25 to 30 minutes, strain and sweeten according to taste with 6 or 7 parts of sugar. Add caramel colouring as desired, cool mixture to 70 degrees C. Add 1 oz. of brewers yeast and allow to ferment for 24 hours. Add a little citric acid to suit the taste: not too much or the lemon flavour will predominate. Let stand for a few days so that it may settle, then bottle.

This product is pasteurized by some manufacturers.

Non-brewed ginger beers became really popular around 1855 and are carbonated drinks with ginger flavouring and usually contain a foam producing ingredient.

Ginger ale is a carbonated beverage produced from ginger ale flavour, sugar syrup, harmless organic acid, potable water and caramel colour. It comes in two types: pale dry and highly carbonated aromatic.

It is an ever popular drink by itself or as a mix with Gin, Scotch or Rye Whiskey. Canada Dry Ginger Ale is one of the most popular of all.

J.J. Mc Laughlin of Toronto was the predecessor of the firm of "Canada Dry".

"CANADA DRY"

John J. McLaughlin, chemist, of Toronto, Ontario, manufactured carbonated beverages in 1890. In 1894 a modern plant was built in Toronto and is still in operation. In 1908 a new ginger ale formula was evolved and placed on the market as "Canada Dry". This proved so popular that the firm built a factory in Edmonton, Alberta, in 1907.

The business was incorporated in 1912 under the name of J.J. McLaughlin Ltd. The sale of Canada Dry in the U.S.A. was begun in 1922 by Canada Dry Ginger Ale Inc., New York, N.Y., producing 500 cases of 50 bottles per day. By 1923 the sales had increased to 103,000 cases per day and a new factory was purchased at Hudson, N.Y.

In Dec. 1923 the issued capital stock of J.J. McLaughlin Ltd. was sold to Canada Dry Ginger Ale Inc., which became the holding company.
Later the Corporation acquired:
Caledonia Springs (Canada) Ltd.
G.B. Seeley's Sons (Canada) Inc.
Chelmsford Ginger Ale (U.S.A.) Inc.

Facts from "Financial Review", 1932.

Above left — Ginger Shandy bottle of J.J. Mc Laughlin Ltd.

Above right — Canada Dry irridescent golden amber bottle.

Left — Ginger Beer Jug — Charles Wilson, Toronto. This firm is still operating and has a number of plants in Ontario.

Above — Three Gurd ginger beer bottles. This firm also manufactured "Aromatic Ginger Ale", "Dry Ginger Ale" and "Aple Flavoured Nectar".

Left to right — Allan's & Co., Ginger Beer, Montreal. Consumer's Ginger Beer Co., Montreal. Fortier & Co., Best Ginger Beer, Quebec. Gurd's Ginger Beer.

CHARLES GURD & CO. LTD.

Charles Gurd & Co., Ltd., were one of the best known manufacturers of ginger beer and other non-alcholic beverages in Canada. First established in May 1868, by 1932 the quality of their products had gained them 3 gold medals, 3 silver medals, 6 bronze medals and 22 diplomas. They received the highest possible awards at such places as The World's Columbian Exhibition-Chicago 1893, World's Fair-Paris, France 1900, The Central Canadian Exhibition-Ottawa 1889.

Left — Three names well known in the Maritimes are shown on these bottles. Most of the bottles used were imported from England and some have the potter's imprint. There were makers of stone bottles in Canada. Some of those used in Nova Scotia and New Brunswick were made by the Munderlon Pottery of Montreal.

Right — Makers of ginger beer also established themselves firmly in British Columbia, Country Club Beverage Co. was one of the better known. Felix Distributors (third from left) also used a glass bottle with "Felix the Cat" as trade mark. Country Club's "Shandy" bottles are rarer than the ginger beer bottles of the same brand.

White unmarked bottle is oriental.

Left — James Roue established his carbonated water business around 1860. There are at least 37 types of James Roue bottles to be found, many of them dated. His son William J. Roue became famous as the designer of the renowned racing schooner "Bluenose".

Extra large bottles from Brandon, Manitoba, firms.

Brandon Brewing Co. used several forms of Beaver trade mark on both their pottery and glass bottles.

E.L. Drewery left no doubt as to the ownership of their bottles.

"King's Old Country" was a popular brand in Manitoba.

Above — Three pottery containers of varied shapes. The "1,875" Victoria Botanic Beverage Co. is rare. The number is not a date. These dispensers for soft drinks were numbered and delivered to the customer on a regular supply basis.

Above and right — Interesting selection of ginger beer bottles. Note the different neck and lip finishes. Brewed ginger beer was an alcoholic beverage.

Colours on pottery bottles range through brown and white, blue and white, green and white, also circular stripes in blue and white. Solid colours seen are - white, buff, light and dark brown.

Above — Two Dr Cronk bottles, example on left marked "Dr Cronk, Port Huron". Also shown a bottle manufactured by Glass Bros & Co., London, Ont.
Bottle on right Wentworth Mineral Water Co., Ltd., Hamilton, Ont.

Farrar's Pottery, StJohns, Quebec, advertised Root and Ginger Beer bottles as early as 1858. It is possible that some of the many manufacturers of ginger beer in Ontario were his customers.

Left — Three bottles from the Hamilton area.

Stone bottle from the F. Meyer
Brewery, Seaforth, Ontario.
These bottles from the collection
of Bill Hart, Seaforth, Ontario.

Label on the above bottle reads:
"The 'Egmondville' Brewery
built originally by Mr George
Weiland. Taken over by the
Colbert family. Closed in 1913".

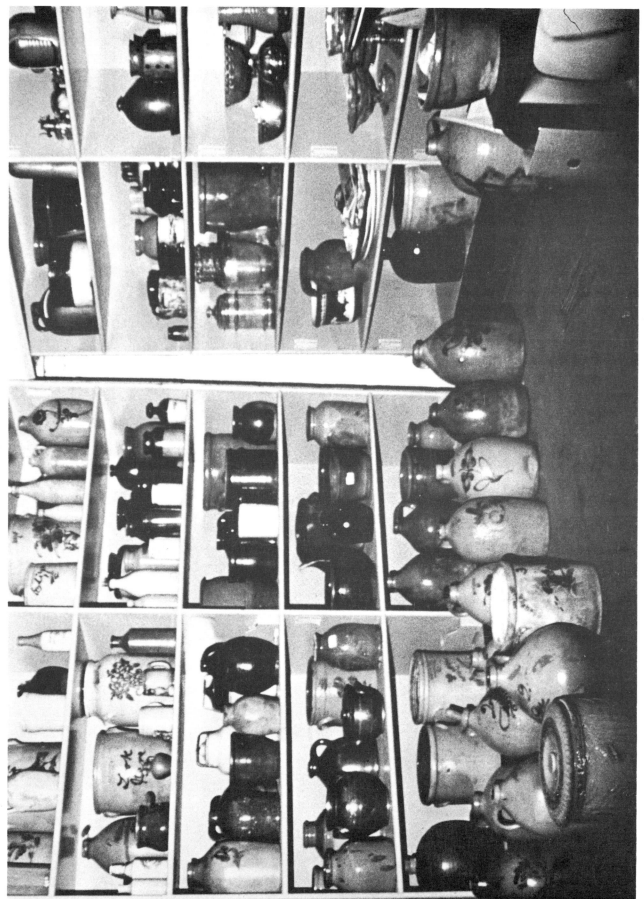

Canadian pottery bottles and containers. Part of the collection of Mr and Mrs Harold Jarvis, Grimsby, Ontario.

CANADIAN

POTTERY

Pottery ink bottles from the collection of George Chopping, Esterhazy, Sask.

Left — An interesting selection of pottery ink bottles. Collection of Mr and Mrs Harold Jarvis, Grimsby, Ontario.

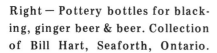

Right — Pottery bottles for blacking, ginger beer & beer. Collection of Bill Hart, Seaforth, Ontario.

A fine example of early Canadian pottery. Four gallon jug with blue finger painting.
Collection of Olga Audet, Quebec.

Canadian pottery bottles from the Hamilton area. Collection of Mr and Mrs Harold Jarvis, Grimsby, Ont.

Canadian pottery bottles from the Egmondville area. Collection of Bill Hart, Seaforth, Ont.

Damaged two gallon jug. Only known example from the Italian Warehouse, Charlottetown, P.E.I.
Collection of Mrs Dennis Campion, P.E.I.

Miniatures made as souvenirs for visitors to the Egmondville Pottery, which was started in 1852 by Valentine Boehler. The pottery closed in 1913.

Jug from the Daniel Orth Potteries of Campden, Ont. Approx. 8 in. high.

There were many potteries in Canada and the story of some of them has already been documented and published in an excellent book "Early Canadian Pottery" by Donald Webster, Curator of the Canadiana Department, Royal Ontario Museum.

Others like the Egmondville pottery near Seaforth, Ontario are being documented and their stories too will be published for all to share.

Medalta Potteries, Medicine Hat, Alberta, were the producers of the three containers — left. A study of jugs used in the area and in Saskatchewan, Manitoba and British Columbia leads us to believe that the pottery manufactured on a large scale, since many examples we have seen seem to be standardized.

Some of the labels (under glaze) found on this type of brown and white jug and also those on other jugs are shown opposite on Page 95.

Below — Stone jug marked "ROOT BEER" with mug inscribed — "CANADIAN DELICIOUS ROOT BEER"

KEY TO LABELS — OPPOSITE PAGE

NAME	SIZES	COLOURS
H.J. Glass	1 gal. & 2 gal.	brown & white
H.J. Glass	¾ gal.	brown & white
Old Corn Liquor	2 gal. & ¾ gal.	brown & white
Davis and Lawrence Co.	2 gal. (bottle shaped)	white & blue
Lavoie & Co.	2 gal. Imp.	brown & white
D.B.W.C.	2 gal. & ¾ gal.	brown & white
J.A. Smith	1 gal. & ¾ gal.	brown & white
Great Western Wine Co.	1 gal. & ¾ gal.	brown & white

It is likely that all were made in three or more sizes from ¾ gal. up.

All drawings of stoneware labels by George Chopping, Parkland Bottle Collectors' Club, Saskatchewan.

H. J. GLASS'
WHOLESALE
WINES & LIQUORS
YORKTON, SASK.

H. J. GLASS
WHOLESALE
LIQUORS
YORKTON, SASK.

GOLD COIN LIQUOR CO.
THE GOOD
WE GET
FROM
GRAIN
MOOSE JAW
CANADA

DAVIS & LAWRENCE CO.
MANUFACTURING
CHEMISTS
MONTREAL AND NEW YORK

LAVOIE & CO.
WINES SPIRITS & CIGARS
25 DUMOULIN ST.
ST. BONIFACE, MAN.

B
D C
W

J. A. SMITH,
WINE MERCHANT.
ESTEVAN.

GREAT WEST WINE CO. LTD.
WHOLESALE
WINES LIQUORS AND CIGARS
Phone M3708
287 Portage Ave. WINNIPEG

Jno. O'Reilly —
brown and white jug

Thos. Jordan —
brown and white jug

A.E. Morrison —
brown and white jug

KEY TO LABELS — OPPOSITE PAGE

NAME	SIZES	COLOURS
Saskatoon Liquor Co.	¾ gal.	brown & white
Woodward Dept. Store	2 gal.	open crock
Western Stoneware	¾ gal.	brown & white
J.F. Cairns	2 gal.	open crock
F. Brotman & Sons	¾ gal.	brown & white
W.M. Ferguson	2 gal.	brown & white
Hudson Bay, Winnipeg	1 gal. & 2 gal	blue & white

It is likely that all were made in three or more sizes from ¾ gal. up.

All drawings of stoneware labels by George Chopping, Parkland Bottle Collectors' Club, Saskatchewan.

SASKATOON LIQUOR CO.

PHONE 220

216 First Avenue

MANUFACTURED
EXPRESSLY FOR
WOODWARD DEPT.
STORES
VANCOUVER, B. C.

WESTERN
STONEWARE

F. L. NEWMAN
WHOLESALE
WINES AND LIQUORS
PORTAGE LAPRAIRIE MAN.

J. F. CAIRNS,
CROCKERY DEPT.
SASKATOON.

E BROTMAN & SONS
WHOLESALE
WINE & SPIRIT MERCHANTS
221-223-225 LOGAN AVE
WINNIPEG, .:. MAN.

W.M. FERGUSON
WINE MERCHANT.
BRANDON MAN.

HUDSON'S BAY CO.
WINNIPEG

MACNAB & ROBERTS
LIMITED
WINNIPEG

97

A group of early "blacks" (1860 — 1890) photographed at Brewery
Creek. These bottles excavated in the Wild Horse area by Mr Rae Masse,
Curator, Fort Steele Museum, British Columbia.

BOTTLES BACK OF BEYOND

by Rae Masse.

How little did they know, those glass blowers of a century ago, that they had created treasures for the future. Their trail can be traced from the earthen vessels found in the middens of the coastal Indians, through the treasures of the Spanish Conquistadors, up the Fraser Canyon to the Yale gold strike of 1858, into the gold fields of the Cariboo during the 1860's, across the Selkirks to the multi-million-dollar gold rush of 1864 on the Wild Horse, to the Telegraph Trail to the Klondike of 1898. An historical travelogue of bottles and broken glass.

Until recently few people knew what an "old" bottle looked like. The difference between a hand-blown-in-the-mould bottle or a machine-made one was a mystery to them. Today there are many bottle hunters in every province and there are those who have become expert and serious bottleologists, knowing where to go and what to look for when they get there.

There is something about the unearthing of old bottles from the ruins and dumps of lost towns and villages, that like digging for buried treasure has an appeal and excitement all of its own. The thrill and satisfaction of bringing up out of the deep folds of old Mother Earth, the hand-molded gem of a "tiger whiskey jug" is, and must be much like that felt by those who drank from its contents or that of the Chinese placermen, when they too dug in the rich gravels and came up with the dull gleaming gold of a rough old nugget!

Have you ever adorned the window sill of your kitchen with purples, greens, gold, cobalt, amber, blues, wheatstraw, blood-red and other varying hues of harmonious bottle colours and watched the early rising sun paint an array of shimmering colour that would bid fair competition to a rainbow or the jewel-like glistening reflections from your light at night casting diamonds, rubies, amethysts and sapphires back into the harmonious arrangement of your comfortable, simple, abode.

Rae Masse at the old Invicta townsite above Fisherville.

Rae Masse Photograph.

Chinese pottery jars. Left—NaKaPy (Tiger Whiskey). Right—preserved onions.

On the natural outcroppings of country rock strewn by ancient glacial drift in my front yard are assortments of purple, cobalt, amber and other hues of glass absorbing the ultra-violet light of the sun's rays. On some huge boulders I have displayed a fantastic array of shapes and colours of old pottery and glass. On others minerals and fossils of all descriptions, even a pile of horns and bones bleaching in the sun in strange yet harmonious contrast.

Inside the rustic cabin I have a more valued rock, mineral and fossil display and more antiquated bottles. Surrounding this as a background are various oils, prints and other pictures. Then there are conversation pieces, knick-knacks of every description, curios, handicrafts, books and writings. This inspiring and leisurely habitat is an ideal retreat for a writer. In these quaint, pleasant surroundings one has time to relax, meditate and think, to read and write and . . . collect bottles.

However, while leading into the satisfying hobby of collecting old, odd and antique bottles let it be established here that this is a comparatively new venture of recreation and cultural accomplishment in the Kootenays, British Columbia and the rest of Canada. From the bottle collectors that I have spoken to and communicated with I have learned that it is catching on at quite a good pace. South of the Border the collecting of bottles has become a highly rated recreational pursuit, and the old dumps and ruins of British Columbia have become a happy hunting ground for many.

On one of the portions of the ancient townsite of Fisherville (Invicta) I have dug down in the rusted remains of an old dump to a depth of barely seeing over the top, standing full upright, all of my half an inch less than six feet. Here one found everything from "Sam-Sooey" jugs, square nails, old boots, preserved and almost petrified bones, to a mustache-mug! You can always tell if you are getting into a Chinese dump by the old shoes, bones and square cans that prevail. And here in this Fisherville site I have found the most concentrated bunch of real old bottles, and some of the best in my collection.

Louie Hollinstein's cabin
on Brewery Creek.

Rae Masse photograph.

The Writer's Retreat on Brewery Creek.

There are such likely places here, yet I have not been able to locate the old bottle dumps, and in some cases I've unearthed old dumps with nothing but rust-eaten cans and other refuse in them, but no bottles. It has been said that some of the old-timers buried their bottles separately in the ground, or dry creek beds. Supposedly they were afraid that the heat of the sun's rays shining through the bottles would ignite fires. I have yet to find one of these treasure-troves.

Tho' like for the mother-lode I keep on looking, digging and hoping.

Over in the Lumberton area, again with my friend, we unearthed some sixty-two (according to her count) tiny "opium" and patent medicine Chinese engraved and embossed bottles. And, here I might inject, it is a good practice to always leave a few bottles for the other guy. In fact, it is not a bad thought to have in mind . . . that you have always left a few for future generations . . . just knowing that perhaps you may have left a few prizes under that last rock or root is a good feeling to have. Don't clean out the last bottle that may be there. That's good sportsmanship. Friendly and more fun that way. There's always another day coming . . . another year. Remember its the rat-race you are getting away from.

There is wealth in the old bottle business, but at this time most Canadians indulge in the happy practice of trading. I suggest you get wise to an enjoyable, interesting and profitable hobby. It will get you away from the rat-race and ease the stress and strain of the fast-moving pace of this semi-automated go-go world. It is in fact a good hobby for the whole family to share. Get out and dig in the old ruins of the mining camps and ghost towns that flourished in our historic province at the turn of the century. There are still fine pieces af Chinese artifacts, antique bottles and other old relics of historic importance to be found.

Rae Masse,
on Brewery Creek,
up Downdraft Gulch,
along the Wild Horse,
out of old Historic Fort Steele,
British Columbia.

This delightfully crooked bottle is a treasured
possession of Mrs D. MacDonald, Moncton, N.B.

IMPERFECTIONS — JUST PERFECT

BOTTLES,
BOTTLES,
BOTTLES

Jeroboams and miniature bottles on display at the new Nova Scotia Museum, Halifax.

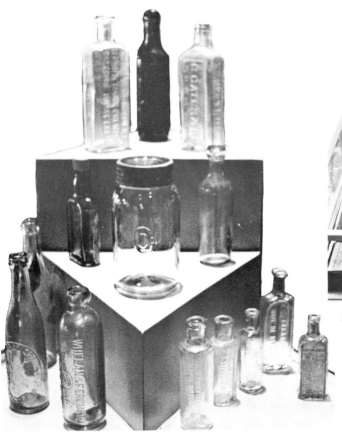

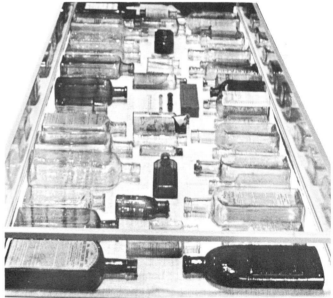

Photographs taken at the new Nova Scotia Museum, Halifax.

LEFT

A miscellany of bottles together with Lamont sealer.

RIGHT

Early medicinals as sold by druggists throughout Canada. Many of the remedies originated in Nova Scotia.

A small part of the collection of Mac Provick, Esterhazy, Sask.

Author Doris Unitt consults Don Mackenzie, collector of bottles for the past eighteen years. A great many of the bottles included in this book were photographed from Don's fabulous collection. He gave generously of his time and advice and also made his extensive library of books and documents available.

Several happy Sunday afternoons were spent at Ye Olde Bottle Shoppe, which Don has at the Fort Edward Flea Market, near Stittsville, on Hwy 7, just West of Ottawa.

108

Above — George Chopping of Esterhazy, Sask., has built an attractive display centre for some of his treasures. The photograph on the opposite page shows recently dug bottles and other items in the Chopping collection.

Bottles on display in Ontario store.

Back room shelves are fully stocked at Nova Nautical Decor, Halifax, N.S.

Authors Doris and Peter Unitt with Bill Hart of Seaforth, Ontario, photographing bottles from his large collection. Personally designed portable studio is used in the production of fine quality pictures (see below).

ABOVE
Three serious collectors of sealers, insulators, bottles and local pottery Graeme Young, David Staffen and Colin Young demonstrate the art of careful digging for the authors.

LEFT
Bottles from this dig gathered together in enamel bowl.

RIGHT
Bottles after cleaning — photographed in colour. See Story Page 115.

A display of early labelled beer bottles together with old fishing prints and Canadian crocks — a small part of the fascinating collection of Bill Hart of Seaforth, Ontario.

BEFORE AND AFTER

Graeme Young, David Staffen and Colin Young, three student friends of Bill Hart took the authors to their own special dig. This is a dump which Bill and his friends have been excavating over the past few months, after it had been closed for fifty years.

Small spade, wooden rake, hand trowel, gloves, if you want to protect your hands, and lots of care combined with patience are needed to dig successfully. In a fairly short time several bottles had been recovered intact plus the enamel bowl, various pottery shards and broken dishes. The boys continued to dig until they filled the bowl, which is shown here with the bottles.

Shown on the opposite page are the same bottles after they had been immersed for two days in sudsy ammonia water, having first been rinsed and emptied of soil and debris. A spout cleanser, tooth brush, nylon pot scourer together with salt and vinegar were used for the final cleansing. Each collector seems to have his own favorite method, but ours worked with this batch very well indeed as can be seen. We were pleased to discover some Canadian bottles in the group, also aqua, dark blue and some turning amethyst. So pleasing did the line-up look that we decided to use it for the cover.

DETAILS OF BOTTLES ON COVER AND PAGE 113

TOP ROW — left to right:

WHISKEY FLASK, clear, double collar, 7½ in. high.

OLIVE JAR, clear, 6 in. high.

BOTTLE, cobalt blue, 8½ in. high, similar to bottle attributed to Como or Hudson Glass Works by Hilda and Kelvin Spence in "A Guide to Early Canadian Glass".

BOTTLE, cobalt blue, applied lip, figure "8" on base, 8 in. high.

LINIMENT BOTTLE, embossed "Bentley's Liniment", Trenton Glass Works, Nova Scotia.

MEDICINE BOTTLE, recessed area on front for label, "D" in diamond on base (Dominion Glass Works Trade Mark), 5½ in. high. Weathering has turned this bottle to a shimmering iridescence.

BOTTOM ROW — left to right:

PERFUME BOTTLE, sun-cast amethyst, Dominion Glass Co. 'Round Lubin' bottle, 3½ in. high.

INK BOTTLE, cobalt blue, applied neck, 3 in. high.

JUICE BOTTLE, sun-cast amethyst, embossed "Welch's" back and front, 5 in high.

INK BOTTLE, square, cobalt blue, embossed "2 ozs" on shoulder at one corner, 2¼ in. high.

PICKLE or PRESERVE JAR, sun-cast amethyst 7½ in. high.

POISON BOTTLE, 3-cornered, aqua, 5½ in. high.

COSMETIC BOTTLE, brown, embossed "Pomade", 2¼ in. high.

SAUCE BOTTLE, aqua-green, embossed "Lea & Perrins" on side,, "Worcestershire Sauce" on shoulder, "NO. 2873" with "K" on base, 7¼ in. high.

MEDICINE BOTTLE, clear, 5½ in. high.

COLOUR GUIDE

Left to right —

TOP ROW

Cornflower blue

Aqua — blue tint

Light blue

Cobalt blue

Purple

Light amethyst

MIDDLE ROW

Emerald

Light green

Amber

Black — green hue

Bottle Green

BOTTOM ROW

Brown

Straw

Black — brown hue

Dark brown

Aqua — green tint

There are many colour variations, but the above are the most often found.

Madonna - wine - Mexico   Moses - Poland Water - U.S.A.   Monkey - wine - Baden, Germany.

Mrs Butterworth - small - U.S.A.   Jug - whiskey - Scotland.   Elephant - ceramic - Japan.

Bottles on display in window of Nova Nautical Decor Ltd., Halifax, Nova Scotia.

Close-up of bottles in right hand corner above taken from inside of store.

An infinite variety is always to be found at Nova Nautical Decor Ltd. —

including ships in bottles, floats, syphons etc.

Avon and other ornamental bottles.

Collection of miniature bottles - reproductions - made by Wheaton, U.S.A.
Others originating in Taiwan — a colourful display where space is limited.

Avon car bottles — modern.

Photograph taken at Fort Steele Historical Museum.

MOULD MARKS

While bottles can be free blown, most are formed in moulds, and, unless made in a turn mould, show the mould marks. Molten glass was blown by lung power into the moulds of wood, metal, or clay, leaving the mould lines imprinted on the glass. On pre-1900 bottles, the mould line does not show on the top or "lip", which was separately shaped and applied after the incomplete bottle was freed from the blowpipe. After 1900, machine-made bottles showed the mould marks over the bottle's full length.

Photograph taken at Fort Steele Historical Museum.

COLOURED GLASS

Glass, in the same way as a cake, can be coloured by its ingredients. The natural shade of most bottle glass was greenish. Glass recipes containing iron slag produced "black glass"; pure gold, a rich ruby red; coal and iron pyrites made ambers; and cobalt gave shades of blue. Some time after 1800, chemicals were added to make a truly "clear" glass. When these bottles were exposed to sunlight, in time they acquired a beautiful pale violet-blue or amethyst tint. This has been referred to as "desert glass" because it was often found near ghost towns where it had lain for years exposed to the direct sunlight.

Pottery or stone bottles from the collection of Larry Griffin, Peterborough, Ontario.

Steigal type bottles circa. 1770.

Miscellaneous group — late 19th century.

Photograph taken at Fort Steele Historical Museum.

WORDS ON GLASS

Bottles with raised lettering or patterns are embossed. The introduction of bottle-making machines around 1900 reduced the number of embossed bottles. While manufacturers continue to put product names and designs on bottles, gone are the nostalgic phrases and preposterous claims of the embossed bottles peddled by old-time travelling medicine men.

Photograph taken at Fort Steele Historical Museum.

POTTERY

These glazed earthenware containers came from China. The graceful urn-shaped and hand-turned jugs held medicinal wines. Other pots and jugs held sauces, preserved fruits and vegetables, fish paste, molasses or similar imported delicacies. Corked or covered with clay lids, then sealed with paper, their contents brought comfort and a taste from home to the Chinese miners living in an alien land.

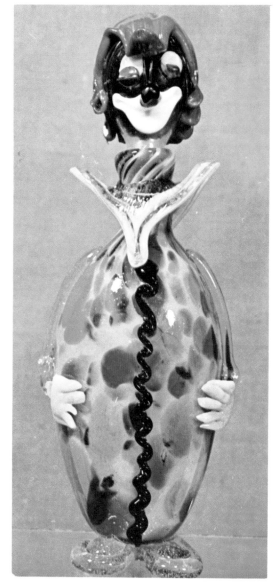

For descriptions of these
bottles — see Page 129.

128

KEY TO BOTTLES ON OPPOSITE PAGE

TOP LEFT; left to right —

Top Row:

Dark green push-up wine bottle, applied lip.

Light green push-up wine bottle, applied lip.

Aqua-green "Pluto Water" bottle, Pluto trade mark on base. Height 12 in.

Aqua-green Irish Whiskey, embossed 'Imperial Quart' on shoulder.

Bottom Row:

Aqua-blue Paine's Celery Compound bottle, embossed name.

Aqua-blue medicinal.

Brown blob top bottle, embossed with name and trade mark of R. Irvine, Montreal.

Aqua-blue, "The Great Shoshonees Remedy of Dr Josephus" embossed. Height 9½ in.

Light blue mineral water bottle, embossed- "Sutherland, Hamilton".

TOP RIGHT —

Italian blown bottle, clown. Height 14½ in.

LOWER LEFT, left to right —

Top Row:

Blob top pottery bottle.

Brewed Ginger Beer bottle, "Milne, Stonehaven, Scotland", Height 9½ in. with stopper.

Blob top pottery bottle.

Bottom Row:

Canadian pottery bottle, Picton, Ont.

Pottery bottle, Russian.

Ceramic Sake bottle, Japanese.

Left — The soap container which is being held by Mr Masse has "Armour's Soap" embossed on both sides. This 18 in. long container is hand blown in three piece mold, with a stone ground mouth opening 5 in. wide. The glass is purpling in a most attractive manner.

Rae Masse, Curator of Historic Fort Steele museum, is shown here in the Drug Store, which was known as the Bleasdale Drug Store in earlier days. It was established 1869 by W. Bleasdale a pharmacist from Fort McLeod, Alberta. On both sides of the building large letters proclaimed "PIONEER DRUG STORE — A.W. Bleasdale, Proprietor". The store carried a wide variety of items as well as medications. Advertisements in 'The Prospector' listed "spectacles, banjo strings, mouth organs, machine and raw oils, meerschaum pipes . . ." etc. etc.

"In fact anything and everything you want --". In 1901 Mr Bleasdale moved to Fernie, B.C. and eventually died there.

On the shelves of the Drug Store today can be found dozens of old time remedies including:

Payco Wine of Pepsin, Canadian Drug Supplies, Vancouver, B.C.

(Many patent medicines were produced in British Columbia)

St Jacob's Oil, Walkerville, Ont. This is in attractive elongated bottles.

Dr Miles Heart Treatment, Toronto, Ont. Many remedies were made by Dr Miles.

A wide range of drugs from Henry K. Wampole Ltd, which is now one of Canada's best known drug supply houses.

Northrop & Lyman Co., Toronto, Ont., offered many products, including Carbolic Acid, which was packed in beautiful cobalt blue poison bottles, heavily embossed with warnings.

Oil of Juniper Wood, from 'Wholesale Druggists', Montreal, Quebec.

Porter's Food, Toronto, Ont. For baby.

Friars Balsam, Martin, Bole & Wynne, Winnipeg, Alberta.

A large selection of local remedies from Beattie-Murphy Co., Ltd., Cranbrook, B.C. Some of the bottles in this selection date back to the original owner of the Company — R.E. Beattie.

There are also a great many English and American products.

LOWER RIGHT, left to right —

Brown case bottle. Height 10½ in.

Barber bottle, D in Diamond mark on base.

Black turn mold bottle.

Green liquor bottle, French.

Part of the collection of Mr and Mrs Dan MacDonald, of Moncton, New Brunswick. Some of the bottles were dug at the site of the old factory of the Havelock Mineral Springs Co. See opposite page.

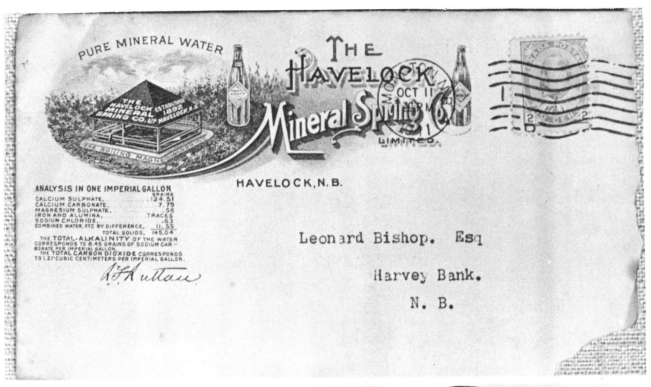

The Havelock Mineral Spring Company was established in 1892. The plant was destroyed by fire in 1895. The firm continued in business in Havelock until 1915, the year in which it moved to Moncton.

Mr and Mrs Dan MacDonald together with Mr and Mrs John MacDonald of Moncton explored and dug at the old Havelock site adding many bottles to their collections. Two of the early bottles are shown on this page. These are — left — dark green and right – aqua, both bottles are 11 in. high.

Two of the later bottles are shown together with molten glass from the burned out factory. These bottles are 8¾ in. high.

The envelope used by the company is one of those interesting additions to a collection, since it not only gives the data concerning the type of bottle used at that time, but the ingredients that went into the making of the contents.

Photograph taken at Radone's Antiques, Amherst, N.S.

VERY RARE WINES FROM PRIVATE CELLARS

(From left to right)
1. Extrait d'Absinthe
2. Old Hock, c. 1780
3. Cape Wine, 1801

4. Canary 1740
5. Cape Wine from (Via) Holland, 1757.
6. Milk Punch 1750
7. Malaga, (Mountain) Prior to 1816

Courtesy Christies, London, England.

The bottles in this advertisement are prior to 1816. Those above are of a later period.

Kingston Whig-Standard, Sept, 1962.

Above — Photograph from the scrap book of Jack Rogers, Peterborough, Ontario.

A group of scuba divers are shown here with bottles and other relics recovered from the cargo of an unidentified ship which was sunk in the St Lawrence near Kingston in the early 1800's.

The young men discovered around 200 clay pipes, barrels of hardware items and cartons of window glass. The containers were rotted through, but most of the cargo had survived.

Careful study of old papers pertaining to local history helps to locate likely spots for diving. However this is a group activity and not one to be entered into in a haphazard manner.

The bottles recovered from the old wrecks are usually the very beautiful blacks, many like those shown here are still sealed and the contents have been in excellent condition.

DON'T BE A PIRATE SCUBA DIVERS WARNED

OTTAWA (UPI)—The federal government has dug out a sea manual which reaches back to pirate days to warn Canada's swelling number of skin and scuba divers.

The warning is spelled out in section 510 of the Canada Shipping act, which was gleaned from the British Merchant Seaman's act of the 1800s, and in those days used to prevent "moonwreckers" from luring merchant ships onto rocky coast lines and looting them.

Unlike the British "moonwreckers" who faced the risk of hanging or deportation if caught, skin and scuba divers are merely being warned by the Department of Transport that a sunken ship and its cargo belongs to its original owner, or in the case of older vessels, to the department. And that the maximum fine for failing to report recovery of a sunken wreck is $400, plus double the value of the wreckage recovered. The fine has not been applied in recent years.

The department wants to insure that historical items brought to the surface by exploring sportsmen end up in Canadian museums.

The warning shown here applies to all parts of Canada.

Lee Jack was one of the first Chinese to invade the Wild Horse diggings, and one of the last to come out. Year in and year out he toiled with gold pan, sluice box and rocker. Sometimes he was rewarded with good sized nuggets and coarse gold, and then again things were not so good. When he had a little bunch of gold accumulated he would come to Cranbrook and dispose of it, buy some grub and a bottle of "lum", as he called it, and again hit back to his shack in the mountain fastness. He died in 1930. *From "Tales of the Kootenays".*

Soy sauce jug.

Top right — Japanese sake bottle with two Chinese bean or preserve jars.

Four "tiger whiskeys" from the Rae Masse collection. Note rare labelled bottle on right.

WILD HORSE AND FISHERVILLE

The history of Fort Steele is inextricably bound up with Wild Horse and the gold rush to that creek. Although David Thompson, early explorer; Father DeSmet, missionary to the Indians; and perhaps one or two other white men, passed through the East Kootenay during the first half of the 1800's, it was the gold discoveries on Wild Horse Creek which brought the white man here in numbers.

In the fall of 1863 a group of miners from south of the border made the journey into the almost unknown area, attracted by reports of gold on Findlay Creek, further north. Though they found little there, they eventually discovered the gold riches of Wild Horse Creek, and by the spring of 1864 the rush was on.

Soon a boisterous shack town sprang up on the lower benches, called Fisherville, after Jack Fisher, one of the original party. The place boasted a population of four to five thousand, although this figure is probably a gross exaggeration. It consisted of miners, laborers, shop keepers, gamblers, saloon keepers and all that goes to make up an early-day mining camp.

The majority of these were from the California gold fields. They celebrated July 4th in true American style, making the most of such as was at hand to give vent to their exuberance and to provide some relief from the grinding work and hardships they endured in the mad search for the precious metal. Consequently they seemed to spend much time either shooting their guns or consuming vast quantities of liquor. This of course did not go down too well with the few British subjects in the camp, but as they were greatly outnumbered, they appear to have made the best of it, and no doubt helped out valiantly in taking care of the liquid refreshments.

When it was realized that the camp was built on very rich placer ground, the buildings, which were mainly hastily thrown up shacks of a temporary nature, were soon either dismantled and moved, or, in most cases, burned down to permit placer operations. The town of Wild Horse then came into being on the higher benches above the creek. Up until around 1900 Dave Griffith ran a store there, also had the post office which was known, not as Wild Horse, but "Kootenay".

At this late date it is impossible to make any accurate estimate of the value of the gold taken out of Wild Horse. It is known that much of it was smuggled across the then loosely guarded international border into the United States to avoid paying royalty, and so of course was never recorded. Unofficial estimates have placed the amount all the way from a most conservative one million to over thirty million dollars. Take your choice. The largest nugget found was alone worth $700.00.

Wild Horse was the seat of government for the Kootenays for about twenty years, during which time the diggings changed from shallow to deep to hydraulicking. By 1882 there were only eleven white miners in the whole of East Kootenay. Somewhere before this time the Chinese flocked to the area and took over much of the diggings, patiently re-working the ground which the white man had hurriedly gone over, then moved on.

The 1890's saw intense hydraulicking and searching for "hard-rock" lode deposits all about the area, and eventually the discovery of the huge silver-lead-zinc deposits at, first the North Star mine, and soon after, the famous Sullivan group at nearby Kimberley. This and Michael Phillipps' discovery of the immense coal deposits in the Crows Nest Pass country gave permanence to the whole area.

Reprinted from "Fort Steele" by permission of Mr Dave Kay, Cranbrook, B.C.

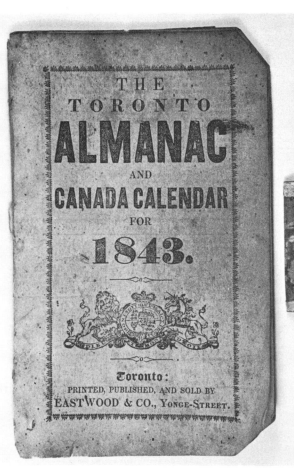

THE TORONTO ALMANAC AND CANADA CALENDAR FOR 1843.

Toronto:
PRINTED, PUBLISHED, AND SOLD BY
EASTWOOD & CO., YONGE-STREET.

HAZELTINE'S
Pocket Book
ALMANAC
1894.
16th Series.
E. T. HAZELTINE,
Warren, Pa.

Dodd's Kidney Pills are a kidney remedy. They strengthen the kidneys so they can do their full work of straining the impurities out of the blood. Dodd's Kidney Pills have been used for backache, diabetes, rheumatism, dropsy, urinary troubles and heart disease. Mr. Joseph Soucy gives the reason why for thirty years Dodd's Kidney Pills have grown in popularity with the people of Canada.

"I got great benefit from the use of Dodd's Kidney Pills. I am satisfied and I want you to tell the people so."

JOSEPH SOUCY,
Mount Joli, Rimouski Co., Que.

AZOR'S TURKISH BALM.

THE GREAT TURKISH REMEDY FOR BALDNESS,
And for Invigorating and Beautifying the Hair.

As a Toilet article for beautifying and keeping the Hair Soft, Glossy, and in a Healthy Condition, it is unequalled. Its restorative qualities are as follows:

1st. It frees the head from dandruff, strengthens the roots, imparts health and vigor to the circulation, and prevents the *hair changing colour* or getting gray.

2nd. It causes the hair to curl beautifully when done up in it over night.

This Balm is made from the original receipt procured from the original Turkish Hakim (physician) of Constantinople, where it is universally used. The Turks have always been celebrated for their wonderful skill in compounding the richest perfumes and all other Toilet articles. In Turkey the *aromatic herbs*, &c., of which this Balm is composed, are almost universally known and used for the hair. *Hence a case of baldness or thin head of hair is entirely unknown in that country.* We wish *but one trial to be made of it*; that will do more to convince you of its virtues than all the advertisements that can be published, and *that all* may be able to test its virtues, it is put up *Large Bottles* at the low price of 50 cents per Bottle.

Remember the *genuine* has the signature of Comstock & Brother on the splendid wrapper.

Twelve Signs of the Zodiac
Aries. Head and Face.

Gemini The Arms
Taurus The Neck
Leo The Heart
Cancer The Breast
Libra The Reins
Virgo The Bowels
Sagittarius The Thighs
Scorpio The Secrets
Aquarius The Legs
Capricornus The Knees

Pisces. The Feet.

NEW MOON — LIBRA or SCALES — VIRGO or VIRGIN — FIRST QUARTER
SCORPIO or SCORPION — LEO or LION
SAGITTARIUS or BOW-MAN — CANCER or CRAB-FISH
CAPRICORNUS or GOAT — GEMINI or TWINS
AQUARIUS or WATER-MAN — TAURUS or BULL
LAST QUARTER — PISCES or FISHES — ARIES or RAM — FULL MOON

LYMAN, SONS & CO.

Henry Lyman.   Henry H. Lyman.   Arthur Lyman.

Original Establishment, Wadsworth & Lyman. 1800.

Wholesale Druggists & Manufacturing Chemists

SPECIALTIES:

Pharmaceutical Preparations, Perfumery, Pure Spices, Chemical, Philosophical and Surgical Instruments.

Office and Warehouse : 384 ST. PAUL ST.   MONTREAL
Drug and Spice Mills, 44 PRINCE ST

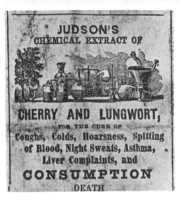

JUDSON'S
CHEMICAL EXTRACT OF

CHERRY AND LUNGWORT,

FOR THE CURE OF

Coughs, Colds, Hoarsness, Spitting
of Blood, Night Sweats, Asthma,
Liver Complaints, and

CONSUMPTION

DEATH

AN UNFAILING REMEDY.

An Hundred Years Testimony.

Dr Roberts'
Ointment
universally known as the
Poor Man's Friend
together with Dr Roberts'
Alterative Pills

WILL TOGETHER CURE THE MOST OBSTINATE OF
WOUNDS, SKIN DISEASES, SCORBUTIC ERUPTIONS.
MARVELLOUS CURES HAVE BEEN WROUGHT.

HALE & HEARTY

Made only by BEACH & BARNICOTT, Ltd., Bridport, Eng.

Zodiacal ANATOMY

The Head and Face
the RAM doth always rule.
The Neck and Throat
are govern'd by the BULL.
O'er the Arms and Shoulders
still the TWINS preside.
Breast, Stomach, Ribs,
the crooked CRAB doth guide.
The noble LION
rules the Back and Heart.
The bashful VIRGIN
claims the Belly Part.
The Reins and Loins
the equal BALANCE weigh.
The SCORPION o'er
the Secret Parts doth sway.
The curious ARCHER
doth the Thighs affect.
So doth the GOAT
our bended Knees protect.
The Legs unto
AQUARIUS' lot do fall.
The FISH our active
feet their portion call.

MEDICINALS

PROMISES! PROMISES!

DON'T SNEEZE!

CANADIAN MEDICINE CO.
MONTREAL, QUE.

BOTTLES IN CANADA

| REFUSE WORTHLESS IMITATIONS |

DOCUMENTS
RESEARCH IS HALF THE FUN

4 TIMES EASIER
TO DIGEST
THAN PLAIN
COD LIVER OIL

THE QUALITY
SCOTT'S
EMULSION

ARIES   LIBRA,
   The Ram   The Scales or Balance
TAURUS,   SCORPIO,
   The Bull   The Scorpion
GEMINI,   SAGITTARIUS,
   The Twins   The Archer
CANCER,   CAPRICORN,
   The Crab   The Goat
LEO,   AQUARIUS,
   The Lion   The Water-Bearer
VIRGO,
   The Virgin
        PISCES, The Fish

Specify "Rigo"

● **PORLIP OVALS**
(the dispensing bottle with the patented lip)

● **DROPPER BOTTLES**
(with the round safety-end pipette, and the seal-tight cap)

● **CAPSULE VIALS**
(clear flint glass without a flaw)

137

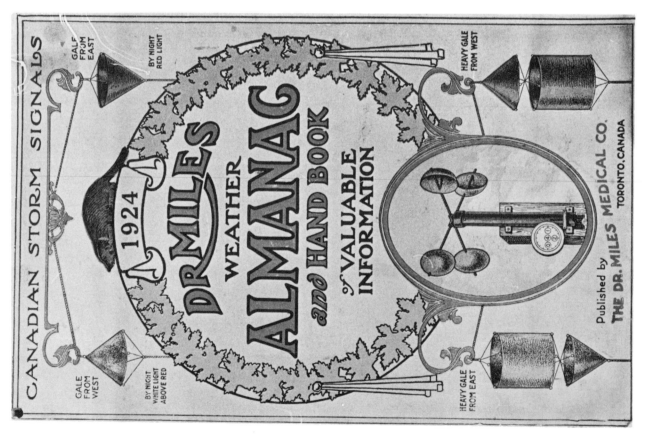

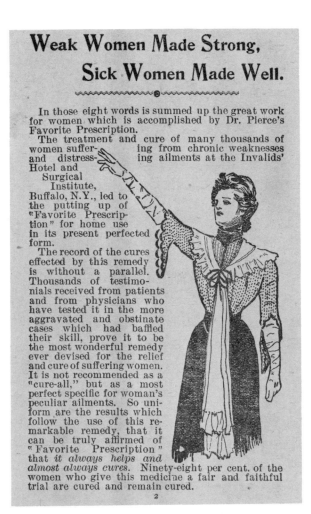
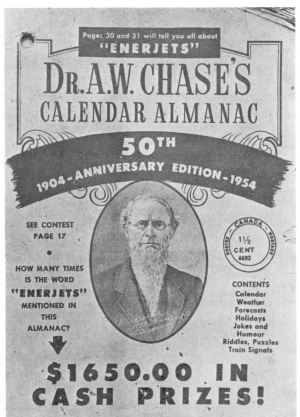
THE ALMANAC

"A book or table containing a calendar of the days, weeks and months of the year, a register of ecclesiastical festivals and saints' days and a record of various astronomical phenomena, often with weather prognostications and seasonal suggestions for the countryman".
is the Encyclopedia Britannica definition of an Almanac.

Printed almanacs date back to the 15th century, but various forms of the almanac have been in use from the days of the earliest astrologers. 'Clog' almanacs made of squares of wood, notched on all four sides, to keep track of the days of the year, were used by Danes and Norwegians and in some parts of England until the 17th century. One Solomon Jarchus is recorded as having prepared almanacs as early as A.D. 1150. Manuscripts of 12th century almanacs are in the libraries of various universities and the British Museum in England.

Perhaps the most famous almanac of all is the "VOX STELLARUM" — "Voice of the Stars", published by Francis Moore in 1700, in which predictions for 1701 were given. Today it is sold as "OLD MOORE'S ALMANAC".

The almanac compiled by William Pierce, mariner for the Harvard College published in Cambridge, Mass., was the first American almanac, and appeared annually from 1639 to 1700.

The Franklin brothers, James and Benjamin both produced almanacs. James published "The Rhode Island Almanac" in 1728. Benjamin, using the name of Richard Saunders, brought out what was to become the best known American publication of this type "Poor Richard's Almanac". This however was outsold by The "Astronomical Diary and Almanac" published by Nathaniel Ames from 1726 to 1775.

The first Canadian Almanac was pub-

Above—Earliest advertisement on this page: from ''Peterboro' Review''; Sept. 20, 1853.

SCOBIE'S CANADIAN ALMANAC for the year 1851 contained a "Catalogue of some of the Economic Minerals and Deposits of Canada, with their localities". The following interesting items appeared under this heading:

HYACINTHS.—Grenville, range 5, lot 10.
AMETHYSTS.—Lake Superior, Spar Island, and sundry places along the neighbouring coast.
RIBBONED CHERT (For Cameos)—Lake Superior—Thunder Bay.
JET.—Montreal.
RUBY }
SAPPHIRE } Burgess, range 9, lot 2 (in minute grains.)

MATERIALS FOR GLASS MAKING.

WHITE QUARTZ SANDSTONE.—Lake Huron—on the north shore, and the Islands near, in great abundance. Cayuga, lots 45 and 46, Town line, north of Talbot road ; Dunn ; Vaudreuil Seigniory. Isle Perrot Seigniory ; Beauharnois Seigniory.
PITCHSTONE, BASALT AND ALLIED ROCKS — (For Black Glass.)—Lake Superior—North shore and Islands ; Michipicoten Island, and East coast. Lake Huron—in the trap dykes of the North shore, and neighbouring Islands. Rigaud mountain ; Montreal mountain ; Montarville mountain.

REFRACTORY MATERIALS.

SOAPSTONE—Elzevir—range 1, lot 27 ; range 2, lot 13 ; Potton, range 5, lot 20 ; Vaudreuil, Beauce Seigniory, range 3 on the Bras ; Broughton, range 4, lot 12.
ASBESTUS—Potton, range 5, lot 20.
SANDSTONE — Lake Huron, Island of Campment d'Ours, west side ; St. Maurice Forges.
PLUMBAGO—Grenville, range 5, lot 10, 2 veins.

Gaspé ; Port Daniel ; Richmond ; Anticosti Island.
LIME— Common—In the various localities above enumerated for limestone Magnesian—In the localities indicated for dolomite. Hydraulic—Point Douglas, Lake Huron ; Cayuga, half a mile and 3¼ miles below the Village, and the Grand River ; Thorold ; Kingston ; Nepean, near Bytown ; Argenteuil ?

MATERIALS FOR BRICKS, TILES AND POTTERY.

CLAY—For Red Bricks—This is so widely spread in the valleys of the St. Lawrence, Ottawa, Richelieu, &c., that the localities are too numerous to be mentioned. For White Bricks—York, range 2 from the Bay, lots 19 and 20 ; Peterborough. For Tiles and common Pottery—All the same localities.

MATERIALS FOR ORNAMENTAL ARCHITECTURE.

MARBLE—White—Dudswell ; exit of Lake Mazinaw, rear of Palmerston (a dolomite.) Black—Cornwall ; Phillipsburgh. Brown — Packenham, at Dickson's mill. Grey and Mottled—McNab ; Phillipsburgh ; St. Dominique ; Montreal. Variegated, white and green —Grenville. Verd Antique—Stukely. Serpentine—In many parts suitable for ornamental purposes, in a range of 135 miles, running through Potton, Bolton, Stukely,

lished prior to 1800. The earliest in the Authors' collection "The Toronto Almanac and Canada Calendar" of 1843 was published by Eastwood & Co, Yonge St., Toronto. This did not carry any advertisements for patent medicines, but was a basic almanac in the accepted sense of the word. The study of later almanacs is most rewarding to the collector, since many were used as a media to promote the medicine man and include many pertinent facts.

Some of the facts we have found in Canadian almanacs:
T. Bickle & Son established Medical Hall in Hamilton in 1835 and still advertised in 1869.
R. Tuton was succeeded by Charles B. Green, druggist, at 80 King St, Toronto, in 1851.
In an almanac put out by John Rankin, Dry Goods Merchant, Dundas, Ontario in 1874, the Victoria Chemical Company offered the consumer:
Victoria Fluid Extract of Buchu and Uva Ursi.
Victoria Compound of Hypophosphites.
Victoria Electric Liniment.
Victoria Carbolic Disinfectant.
Victoria Glycerine Jelly in bottle and various other salves and remedies.
Dr Chase established his business in 1864, but did not publish his Almanac until 1904.
The Canadian Almanac 1867 reveals the fact that George Woods registered under Canadian Patents "A new and useful medicine", which he named "Wood's Unrivalled Canadian Pain Killer". The same almanac included advertisements for Perry Davis's Vegetable Pain Killer, which had already been on the market for seven years and an advertisement for "The Challenge", a Temperance paper started in 1854.
The "Spectator" Canadian Farmers' Almanac of 1868 was using the Signs of the Zodiac indicating the various parts of the anatomy the signs controlled. For the first time the calendar page was

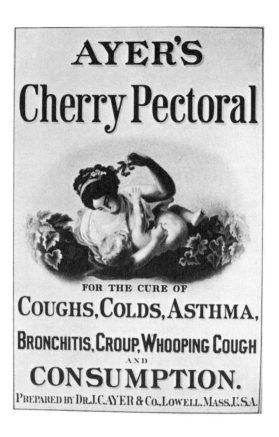

Local Historical Societies can be most co-operative. Your local library may have old directories tucked away. The Public Archives in your Province is likely to have Canadian Directories on microfilm.

Researching your collection is almost half the fun.

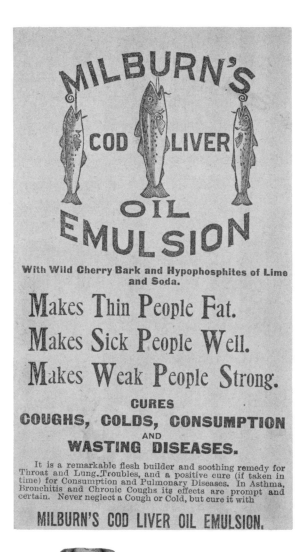

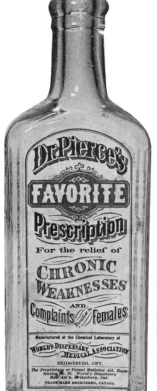

See Page 139 for Advertisement.

adapted and calculated for the whole country.

Thos. Lawrence & Co. of Hamilton prepared prescriptions and family recipes.

T. Morson & Son of London, England, offered New Medicinal Preparations, including Saccharated Wheat Phosphates, Creosote, Pancreatic Emulsion, and Pepsine Wine.

W.W. Kitchen was a Wine Maker at Grimsby in 1868.

Ontario Vineyard, owned by Henry Bauer, offered Native Grape Wine during the 1860's.

The tax on olive oil was one shilling per gallon in 1881.

Parke & Parke Ltd was started in 1892 and published an almanac to promote their many products.

Burdock Blood Bitters was the product of T. Milburn of Toronto and bottled by his firm in Canadian bottles. Milburns offered an almanac in the form of a pocket memorandum book. The 1892 edition advertises old favorites like Dr Fowler's Extract of Wild Strawberry with the question "How Much Is Your Baby Worth?" — "Worth Its Weight In Gold". The syrup, not the baby. Hagyard's Pectoral Balsam at 25 cents was proclaimed to be "The Most Pleasant and Perfect Throat and Lung Healer in The World"; and Dr Low's Worm Syrup is described as "Pleasant".

T. Milburn also had his own selection of medications and his advertisement for "Cod Liver Oil Emulsion" is shown here.

Most bottles of this period were embossed and/or labelled and by checking through old almanacs and early directories the history of the medication and manufacturer can often be traced.

Besides using almanacs check old newspapers, directories, early magazines, advertisements and of course catalogues are valuable. Trade associations can be helpful if approached properly and given time to answer your questions.

Letters to firms should be addressed to the Director of Public Relations with the request he pass it to the man most likely to have knowledge of the subject.

Above —
This green bottle may also be seen in colour section Pages 113 — 128.

Advertisements from the "Canadian Lancet", and other 19th century publications.

Oil, Castor, 4 oz, 15c per bottle.
Oil, Castor, 8 oz, 25c per bottle.
Oil, Black, "Darley's," 25c per bottle.

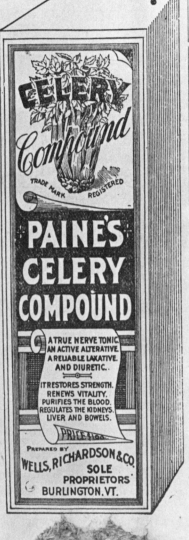

CELERY Compound
TRADE MARK REGISTERED

PAINE'S CELERY COMPOUND

A TRUE NERVE TONIC
AN ACTIVE ALTERATIVE
A RELIABLE LAXATIVE
AND DIURETIC.

IT RESTORES STRENGTH.
RENEWS VITALITY.
PURIFIES THE BLOOD.
REGULATES THE KIDNEYS,
LIVER AND BOWELS.

PRICE $1.00

PREPARED BY
WELLS, RICHARDSON & CO.
SOLE PROPRIETORS
BURLINGTON, VT.

CAUTION!

To prevent the substitution of SPURIOUS IMITATIONS for the genuine articles, by unprincipled Shopkeepers —a SMALL COPY of each article as it appears in its wrapper, is here annexed.

ROWLANDS' MACASSAR OIL for promoting the Growth, the Restoration, and for Preserving and Beautifying the Human Hair. For Children it is invaluable, as forming the basis of a Beautiful Head of Hair. Price 3s. 6d., 7s., 10s. 6d. (equal to 4 small) and 21s. per bottle.

ROWLANDS' KALYDOR for Improving and Beautifying the Skin and Complexion, eradicating all Cutaneous Eruptions, Sun-burns, Freckles, and Discolourations, and for rendering the Skin soft, clear and blooming. Price 4s. 6d. and 8s. 6d. per bottle.

ROWLANDS' ODONTO, or Pearl Dentifrice, for imparting a Pearl-like whiteness to the Teeth, and strengthening the Gums, and for giving a delicate fragrance to the breath. Price 2s. 9d. per box.

WHOLESALE AGENTS:—For MONTREAL—Messrs. Carter, Kerry & Co., and Messrs. Lyman, Clare & Co —for QUEBEC: Mr. F. Royse —and for TORONTO: Messrs. E. Hooper & Co. Sold Retail by all respectable Chemists and Perfumers.

Pre-1900 advertisements from almanacs, catalogues and newspapers.

From Death to Life.

We especially recommend Radam's Microbe Killer to that class of people who have tried other remedies in vain. Thousands upon thousands of hopeless and despairing sufferers have been completely restored to health and strength, and are being cured by this wonderful remedy. We could fill volumes with the names of persons who have been cured by using this remedy; cases, too, who were prostrated by extreme debility, discouraged, disheartened, many of them pronounced incurable by physicians and given up to die. It destroys all the germs of disease.

If your druggist or local storekeeper hasn't got it in stock, he can get it for you, or we will send it to you direct. Write to us.

THE RADAM MICROBE KILLER CO., LONDON, ONT.

PERUVIAN SYRUP
AN IRON TONIC
FOR DYSPEPSIA — DEBILITY — DROPSY — HUMORS

NATURE'S OWN VITALIZER

CAUTION.—All genuine has the name "Peruvian Syrup," (NOT "Peruvian Bark,") blown in the glass. A 32-page pamphlet sent free. J. P. DINSMORE, Proprietor, 36 Dey St., New York. Sold by all Druggists

145

The fascination of old newspapers is endless. These ads from 1871 issues of the Lindsay "Victoria-Warder" reveal the fact that Teas and Liquors were really big business in those days. Note the remark in the Frank Munro ad "He has within the past few weeks, received over $3,000 worth of Teas and Liquors alone". Also note "He buys them for cash down and is thus enabled to sell cheap".

The "Pure Liquors for Medical Purposes" in the Dobson & Niblock advertisement gives one a clue to the medical practices of that time.

VICTORIA BREWERY,
WILLIAM ST., LINDSAY, ONT.,
TATE & BELL - PROPRIETORS.

The subscribers beg leave to notify the public that they have opened business in the above line in the building formerly occupied by J. C. Rodden, where they intend brewing

Ales and Porter of the Best Quality!

MR. TATE being a PRACTICAL BREWER from one of the Leading Houses in England, the public may depend upon receiving an article superior to anything ever before brewed in Victoria.

Orders by Mail or otherwise promptly attended to.

Address all Orders—

TATE & BELL,

611

BOX 124, LINDSAY, ONT.

ROBT. TATE.

R. G. BELL.

DOBSON & NIBLOCK,
KENT STREET, LINDSAY,

Wholesale & Retail Dealers in

TEAS, TOBACCOS, WINES, BRANDIES, LIQUORS,

And General Groceries,

Beg to announce to their customers and the public that their stock is now full and complete.

TEAS, selected with the greatest care, and of the finest qualities.

TOBACCOS, of all kinds.

Wines, Brandies, Choice Whiskeys, Ale & Porter,

Of the best known Brands.

INVALIDS in want of **PURE LIQUORS** for Medical purposes will find them with us.

TO COUNTRY MERCHANTS, HOTEL KEEPERS & LUMBERMEN, we offer goods on the most favorable terms.

DOBSON & NIBLOCK,

Groceries, Groceries, Groceries !
Liquors, Liquors, Liquors ! !

THE subscriber has great pleasure in again calling the attention of his numerous friends, and the public, to the immense increase which he has lately made to his already large and well assorted stock of Groceries and Liquors, which will be found, on inspection, to be the Largest and Best Stock ever seen in Lindsay, and rarely surpassed by any but large city houses. As his customers are already aware, he makes Teas and Liquors a speciality. Country and other Merchants are supplied on the most liberal terms. He has, within the past few weeks, received over $3,000 worth of Teas and Liquors alone. The best judges of Teas in Lindsay say that nothing equal to the delicious flavor of his Teas has ever been known here before. He has imported PICKLES, SAUCES AND CATSUPS in endless variety. Among his Liquors will be seen any quantity of

GOODERHAM & WORTS' A 1 MALT AND RYE,

In Quality and Quantity equaled by none ever before brought into Lindsay. He buys them for cash down and is thus enabled to sell cheap. Also on hand, large quantities of Hennesay's Brandy, Irish and Scotch Whiskeys, English Ale and Porter, and superior Port and Sherry Wines, and Brandies. He would say to Country Merchants, Saloon Keepers, and the public generally, that a call at the

"House of All Nations"

Will soon convince them of the entire truth of what is above stated.

FRANK MUNRO.

GREAT SHOSHONEES REMEDY

On the opposite page is an advertisement from the Lindsay "Victoria Warder" of Jan 18, 1871.

It is especially interesting for several reasons. The wording of the ad. implies that this is a Canadian remedy. No reference can be found in books on the Canadian Indian to any Shoshonees in British Columbia.

In a recent letter to the authors Mac Provick of Esterhazy, Sask. says "I took out my 'Indians of Canada' by Diamond Jenness and they are not mentioned. So I took out an old encyclopedia reference and found that the Shoshone are one of the great divisions of the Great Plain Indians once roaming from Idaho to the Gulf of Mexico and from Montana to the coast".

Mr Provick also commented on the "Large Pints $1.00 . . . this is no doubt the ancestor of the 'Jumbo Half Quart' that the U.S. Government recently cracked down on".

It would be of value to locate a handbook, almanac, treatise or circular about this product to better ascertain who was the proprietor. The phrase "wholesale agents" could indicate that this was an American product dressed up for the Canadian market.

PROCLAIM THE GLAD TIDINGS!

That the GREAT SHOSHONEES REMEDY AND PILLS, of the eminent Indian *Medicine-Man*, DR. LEWIS JOSEPHUS, of the Great Tribe of Shoshonees, British Columbia, is working the most marvelous and astonishing cures the world ever heard of. Never in the annals of Canadian Medical History has such success attended the introduction of any medicine heretofore.

WHY?

Simply because the numerous valuable active medicinal vegetable ingredients (some of which we will mention, such as the extracts of Wild Cherry Bark, Podophyllum, Juniper, Quassia, Smartweed, Dandelion, Hyoscyamus, Compound Extract of Colocynth, Jalap, Socotrine Aloes, Capsicum, etc., etc.) which enter into the composition of the combined medicine, are such and so harmoniously classified and compounded, that it is made the most searching curative in the known world, and cannot help but act on the system in a very satisfactory and desirable manner. No matter what your ailment may be, or of how long standing, it will find the spot and astonish you by the rapid manner in which you are restored to perfect health and full vigor.

This Medicine is pleasant and safe to take, and is warranted, and may positively be relied upon to make a permanent cure of all diseases of the Throat Lungs, Liver, Kidneys, Digestive Organs, etc., as well as Scrofula, the various Skin Diseases, Humors and all diseases arising from Impurity of the Blood, excepting the Third Stage of Consumption. Further information, with full directions for using the Great Shoshonees Remedy and Pills, and containing Testimonials and Certificates of Cures, can be obtained by securing the Treatise, the Hand-book, or the Almanac and Circulars from any respectable Druggist in the Dominion—free.

Price of the Remedy in Large Pints, $1
Pills per Box, 25 Cents.

For sale by all Druggists. and Dealers in Medicine
☞ Agents for Lindsay. — Messrs. E. Gregory Coulter & Son, Thirkell & Perrin, and Northrop & Lyman, wholesale Agents.

147

EXHIBITS OF SIMPSON, HALL, MILLER & CO., SILVER-WARE, WALLINGFORD CT. BRANCH, MONTREAL.

EXHIBITS OF H. SUGDEN EVANS & CO., WHOLESALE DRUGGISTS, OF MONTREAL.

EXHIBITS OF JOHN HENDERSON & CO., FURRIERS, OF MONTREAL.

OTTAWA.—THE FIRST DOMINION EXHIBITION.

Bottom left – H. Sugden Evans & Co. had large display of
their well known lines including "Monserrat Juice of Lime".

LAMPLOUGH & CAMPBELL,

CHEMISTS AND DRUGGISTS, NEXT TO THE COURT-HOUSE, MONTREAL.

IMPORTERS OF

ENGLISH & FOREIGN DRUGS, CHEMICALS, PATENT MEDICINES, SURGICAL INSTRUMENTS, PERFUMERY

AND DRUGGIST'S SUNDRIES.

MANUFACTURERS OF PHOTOGRAPHIC CHEMICALS

AGENTS FOR

Keating's Cough Lozenges & Anthelmintic Bon-Bons, Decastro's Hydrate of Magnesia, Howard's Suc-
cedaneum and Tooth Powder, Rimmel's Toilet Vinegar and Perfumery, &c., Phillips' White Wax—
Warranted Pure, DuBarry's Revelanta Arabic Food, Pulvermacher's Hydro-Electric Chains.

In addition to a well selected Stock of Drugs and Chemicals, the subscribers have constantly on hand

Pure Essen. Oils & Colog. Spirit.	Honeysuckle Soap	*Finest Quality, Eng.& French*—	Tortoise Shell Combs, rich pat-
Lubin's Extracts, 65 varieties.	Glycerine "	Hair Brushes, 150 patterns.	terns, and in great variety.
Cosmetiques.	Sand Tablets, "	Cloth "	Buffalo Horn Combs.
Bandolines.	Winter and Thompson's Rypo-	Flesh "	India Rubber "
Pomades.	phagon.	Tooth and Nail Brushes.	Horn "
Fancy Soaps in great variety in-	Patey's Transparent Soaps.	Badger Hair Shaving "	Fine Ivory "
cluding—	Bayley's Spermaceti Tablets and	Turkey, Trieste and Venetian	Puffs and Puff Boxes.
Trinder's Finest Honey Soap.	Ess. Bouquet.	Sponges, direct importations.	Nipple Shells, Shields & Teats.
Brown Windsor "	Hooper's Cachous.	Alpaca and other Sponge Bags.	India Rubber Rings.
Musk "	" Pastilles.	Toilet Bottles, direct from	Feeding Bottles.
Rose "	Jean Marie Farina's Finest Col.	Frankfort.	Breast Pipes.
Honey and Almond "	Jos. Ant. " in Wicker.	Silver Mounted Smelling Bot-	" Pumps.
Sunflower "	Rose and Orange Flower Water.	tles, English and French.	Toilet Powder.

Surgical Instruments, Enema Apparatus, Glass and Metal Syringes, Trusses, Suspensory Bandages, Magnetic
Apparatus, Medicine Chests, Pill Boxes, Tooth Powder do., Lip Salve do. wood and china, Graduated
Measures, Mortars, Pill Knives, Counter Scales, Funnels, Pill Tiles, Soda Water Tumblers,
Cold Cream Pots, Bears Grease do., Fancy Labels, Wax Matches, English and Ger-
man Night Lights, Camel Hair Pencils, Cox's Gelatine, French do. Oil'd
Silk, Fine Colored Twines, Tin Foil, Daguerreotype Chemicals,
English and French Confectionery, &c., &c.

PROPRIETORS OF SAVAGE'S URSINA.

Montreal, October, 1857.

Chemists' and druggists' lists are a fascinating area in which to research bottle history.

GENUINE MEDICINE WAREHOUSE,

DANIEL'S BLOCK, OPPOSITE STRONG'S HOTEL,

DUNDAS STREET, LONDON, C. W.

EDWIN HEATHFIELD,

HAVING resolved to stand unrivalled in every Department of HIS business, has agreed with the
Proprietors and Agents of all the Genuine Popular Patent Medicines throughout the United
States, to keep him constantly supplied with a fresh and ample Assortment, at Rates FAR below the
usual Market Prices.

By this arrangement Mr. H. is enabled to offer for the inspection of purchasers, THE MOST
EXTENSIVE Assortment which can be found in this or any other city.

Having had many years experience in the sale and purchase of Patent Medicines, Mr. H. has
acquired facilities for conducting this particular department, on the most liberal scale, and is now prepared to supply the Trade at Prices SO EXCEEDINGLY LOW, that the purchaser cannot fail to realise a
handsome per centage on his investment.

At Wholesale at his Establishment may be found a full Assortment of

ALL GENUINE PATENT MEDICINES, ESSENTIAL OILS,

GROCER'S DRUGS, &C.

PRINTER'S INK OF ALL COLOURS, ALWAYS ON HAND.

London, C. W., September, 1857.

Note the cut-rate come-on in this advertisement.

Canadian drug store of the 1860's.

Hudsons Bay Company Winnipeg Store, from the cover of their 1899 catalogue.
The Company has been adding to the bottles in Canada for over 300 years.

A DRINK THAT CHEERS & STRENGTHENS

THERE IS

REAL

ENJOYMENT

AS WELL AS

SOLID

BENEFIT

IN A CUP

OF

JOHNSTON'S

FLUID

BEEF.

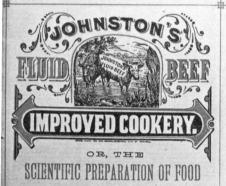

JOHNSTON'S FLUID BEEF

IMPROVED COOKERY.

OR, THE

SCIENTIFIC PREPARATION OF FOOD

Has lately occupied some public attention, and it may be anticipated that a more general knowledge of the chemical composition, preparation, and physiological effects of food will be the result. In this connection we submit the latest theory for the preparation of a perfect beef tea or "hygienic food," and in soliciting a perusal, trust it may prove not uninteresting.

Every vital action, mental or muscular, is accompanied with a proportionate waste in the structures of the body, and to renew this continuous waste is the ultimate design of all food. In order that food may be thus transformed into the various parts of the living organism, it is first essential that the materials of such structures shall be contained in the food supplied, for the human system is absolutely incapable of producing muscular fibre, cellular tissue, blood, brain, bone, etc., out of substances which do not contain the elements of which those organs are composed. And in proportion as food contains such elements in an available form, so is it termed nutritious or otherwise. Extract of Meat, or Beef Tea, is everywhere acknowledged as a harmless stimulant, serviceable in prostration, or as an adjunct to easily digested food; but outside medical or scientific circles it is not generally known that such extracts are simply the flavor of meat (technically the soluble salts of flesh), and as such are not in any real sense nutritious. In this connection we quote from the standard authorities, Drs. Edward Smith, H. Letheby, and Baron Liebig:

In the paper read by Dr. EDWARD SMITH before the British Association, August, 1865, he says of Meat Extract: "When, therefore, you have excluded fat, fibrine,

JOHNSTON'S FLUID BEEF is now extensively used in British and Continental institutions, Hospitals and Asylums, and is prescribed by the medical faculty wherever it has been introduced.

Its adaptability is general to the invalid, the convalescent and the vigorous. To children it secures a strong muscular development, and for maternal nursing, imperfect mastication, athletic training, physical exhaustion, indigestion or mental overstrain, it is the perfection of known food.

DIRECTIONS FOR USE.—Add a small teaspoonful to a cup of boiling water and season to taste ; or as a sandwich paste it may be used on toast, with or without butter. The can may remain open for weeks without detriment to the contents.

Sold by Druggists and Leading Grocers. Price 35c, 60c, & $1.

Robert Shoemaker & Co., Philadelphia. General Agents, U. S.

LOCAL AGENTS : W. H. SCHIEFFELIN & CO., WM. ST., NEW YORK.
CUTLER BROS. & CO., BROAD STREET, BOSTON.
THOMSEN & MUTH, BALTIMORE, Md.

Manufactured by JOHN L. JOHNSTON, Montreal, Canada.

Johnston's Fluid Beef was a Canadian product which achieved world wide recognition. Its nutritional value was praised in England in the early 1870's. The analyst's report stated "It is one of the most perfect foods I have ever examined". It was even prescribed by Queen Victoria's Physician, Dr Thomas Watson.

Syr. Hypophos. Co., Fellows.

Many druggists and doctors of 19th century Canada prepared their own formulas and advertised them widely in the papers of the day. James I. Fellows, Chemist, became known throughout the world for his "Fellows' Syrup of Hypophosphites".

Advertisements in the "Canadian Lancet" during the 1880's and 1890's show that he had offices in Canada, America and England. On bottles made for this product is embossed "Fellows & Co., Chemists, St John, N.B." This firm was one of the largest customers of the Trenton Glass Works. Whether bottles were manufactured for them elsewhere has not been ascertained.

In the authors' collection is a Fellows bottle which was dug up in street excavations at the time of the dismantling of London Bridge and brought back to Canada by Mr Richard Smythe of the Hamilton Market. The bottle has become quite irridescent and was obviously buried for a long period. Fellows produced other medications but none became as famous as the Hypophosphites.

J.D.B. Fraser, Druggist, of Pictou, N.S. had many competitors in the making of remedies containing cod liver oil and his product did not have the same appeal as Scott & Bowne's "Perfect, Permanent, Palatable" emulsion, that came in a bottle embossed with a man carrying a fish as big as himself.

—CONTAINS—

The Essential Elements to the Animal Organization—

Potash and Lime :

The Oxidizing Agents—Iron and Manganese ;

The Tonics—Quinine and Strychnine ;

AND

The Vitalizing Constituent—Phosphorus,

Combined in the form of Syrup,

with Slight Alkaline Reaction.

Fellow's Formula, as advertised in the "Canada Lancet", October 1883.

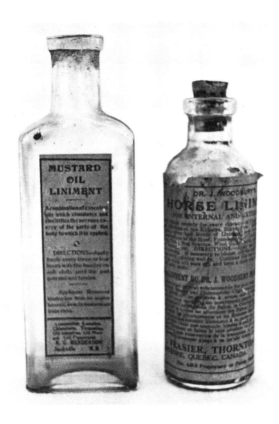

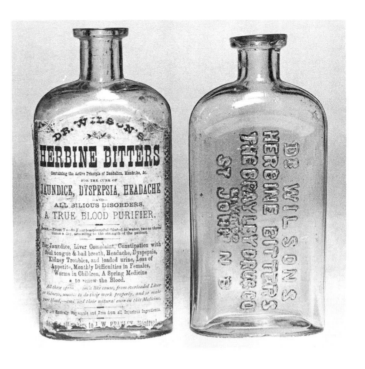

The doctors and druggists of Canada were not slow to offer remedies and cures to a public eager for medication.

Above — left and right — four bottles from the Trenton Glass Works. Note — bottles would be embossed to match label. i.e. a Montreal distributor would have a matching address embossed.

Below — Note the Beaver in the Evans & Sons trademark on the "Ladies' Slipper" bottle.

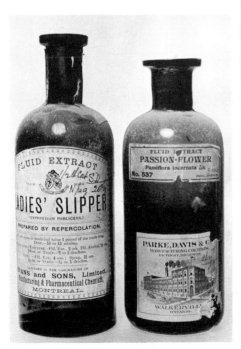

Many familiar names have been around for several decades. Clear, blue or amber bottles which contain their products have changed their shape only slightly

153

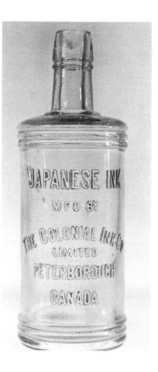

Bottle embossed–
Sirop des Enfants
du Dr Coderre.

NO—MO—ODO
prepared by Morse,
Toronto.

Ink bottle —
embossing as shown.

Bouey Bros Co,
Winnipeg.

Note — sometimes the embossing is painted before photographing to make it more readable.

A selection of embossed "Ozone" bottles,
all sun-cast amethyst. Left to right —
1. Liquizone.
2. The Ozone Co. of Toronto, Ltd.
3. The National Drug & Chemical Company
   of Canada Ltd.
4. T. Kennedy, Hamilton, C.W.

Above —
Eno's Fruit
Salts. 2 oz.
size.

Colour adds to the
value of bottles. This
Ozone bottle is dark
amber — 9 in. high.

154

A selection of bottles from Canadian glass works. The attractive cobalt blue bottles were used by manufacturing chemists and drug stores right across the country and are of more interest and value if they are still labelled. The small essence bottles can readily be found, but usually without labels.

POINTS TO REMEMBER

1. Colour and shape are important.

2. Values increase according to rarity.

3. Condition is a factor when pricing.

4. Embossing is desirable on medicinals, minerals, spirits and beers.

5. Beautifully blown bottles of the 18th century are the collector's choicest find.

Medicinals in varied shapes, sizes and colours — pale aqua to cobalt blue, at Nova Nautical Decor, Halifax, Nova Scotia.

Bottles from the Sovereign Perfume Co., Toronto.

Left to right back row — Cobalt blue cathedral type pickle, 7 in. high.
Blue, embossed — Bromo Seltzer, Emerson Drug Co, Baltimore, Mass.
Three cornered poison bottle, aqua. 'Picnic' shape flask.
Front row — Mucilage bottle, clear. Miniature Bromo Seltzer,
blue, 2¾ in. high. Blue 'Druggist' bottle.

Two bottles from Evans & Sons,
Manufacturing Chemists, Montreal.
Beaver trade mark.

Left — Amber 'patent medicine bottle'.
Centre — Blue unmarked bottle.
Right — Two essence bottles. Tallest of
the two 6½ in. high.

LABELS ARE IMPORTANT

Bottles were not cheap and many manufacturers would refill those they could obtain with products other than the original contents. The three bottles above are typical examples of this practice.

DO NOT DESTROY LABELS WHEN CLEANING BOTTLES

Many bottles like these have been found without labels and many are lost in cleaning. Labels are valuable aids to discovering the uses to which bottles were put and in identifying firms of the area in which they are found or from which they have come. The value of the bottle is increased if the label belonged to a firm which existed for a short period only. Some firms used a variety of labels and collecting a set of their labelled bottles can be interesting and rewarding, A typical example of varied labelling is that of F.M. Pilgrim of Brockville, Ont., and Aylmer, Que.

Recently Kaye McFarland of Napanee purchased some bottles for resale in her store and to her horror when the owner arrived with them she apologised for being late saying "I didn't realize it would take me so long to soak the labels off, but I've got them all clean for you".

Above — two 4 in. bottles.
Bottle on left embossed:
Waterbury Battery Oil
Waterbury Manufacturing Co
Perth, Ontario.
Made in Canada
Bottle on right embossed:
Edison
Battery Oil
Made in U.S.A.
Thomas A. Edison
Incorporated
Bloomfield, N.Y.

Left — Radnor Springs Mineral Water.
Centre — Wine bottle reused.
Right — "Duncan Water" in cobalt blue
bottle was produced by the Caledonia
Springs Company Ltd., which was later
purchased by Canada Dry Ltd.

Above — Bovril bottles are found
coast to coast and range in size
from 1 oz. to 16 oz.

Left —
Garland & Rutherford
Apothecaries
King St
Hamilton
Note elaborate monogram.

Above — Canadian, French and American bottles. Embossed as shown. Tallest 7 in. high.

Right — Nova Scotia and New Brunswick medicine bottles. Embossing as shown. Tallest 7½ in. high.

Left — Collection of blue bottles. Tallest 8½ in. high.

Left —
Group of medicinals.
Left to right —
(1) Anti Diputheritique
(2) Lyman Sons & Co.
Manufacturing Chemists
Established 1849, Montreal
(3) Sirop Gartier
(4) Prepared by Dr Peter
Fahrnet & Co, Winnipeg, Man.
(5) Diphterine

Right —
(1) Barrel shape bottle.
(2) Food or pickle jar.
(3) Embossed "Cocoa Glycerine".
(4) Amber medicinal bottle.

Left — selection of blue bottles.
Left to right —
(1) Embossed: Nuskin Co.
(2) Blue ink.
(3) No markings. 7½ in. high.
(4) Embossed: Carbolic Acid,
use with caution.
(5) & (6) Two sizes of poison,
embossed: caution, be careful
& external use-use with caution.

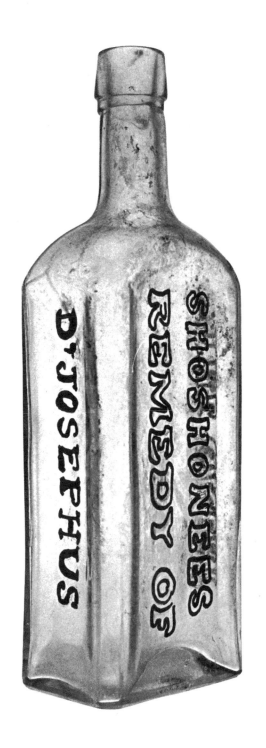

Aqua one pint bottle.
The Great Shoshonees Remedy.

The Dispensary, Fort Steele, British Columbia.
Below — four druggist bottles, collection of George Chopping.

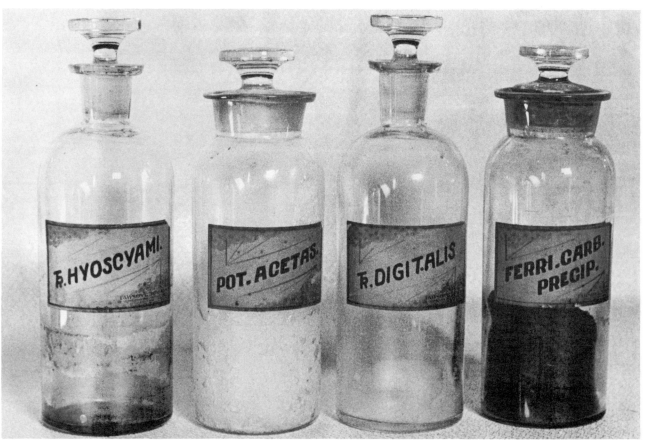

MANY SHAPES AND SIZES

Top — miniature liquor bottles with 7 in. square blue-green Italian bottle.
Bottom — bottles from ¾ in. high to 17 in. high.

Miniatures which include H.P. Sauce, Holbrook's Worcestershire Sauce, Rose's Lime Juice, Johnson's American Liniment. Tallest bottle 7½ in., shortest 2½ in.

Miniature bottles — back row — ink bottle, play candy bottle, medicinal. Front row — Avon perfume, mini Coke bottle, medicinal. Bottles life size.

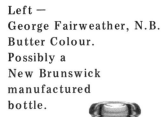

Left —
George Fairweather, N.B.
Butter Colour.
Possibly a
New Brunswick
manufactured
bottle.

Right —

Johnston's Fluid Beef.
was used in Canada,
England and America.

Amber bottle
Several sizes

The number
and variety
of shapes
combined
with
interesting
embossings
makes the
collecting of
soft drink
bottles
a challenge.

Old time remedies. Full bottles in
unopened packages are very desirable.

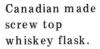

Canadian made
screw top
whiskey flask.

THE PACKAGE ADDS INTEREST

Authors' collection.

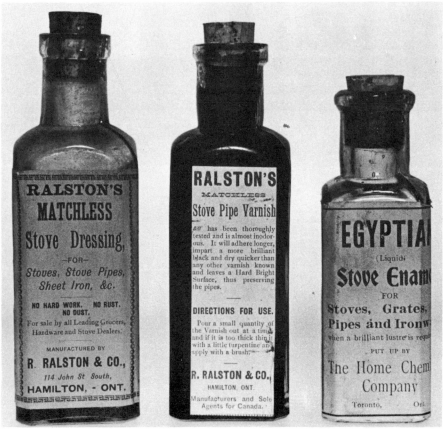

Authors' collection.

Richards Glass Co., Toronto, was established in 1912 and are distributors of Dominion Glass Co. products.

Many bottles were produced for them from their own molds — on these the "Rigo" or "R.G. Co. T" symbols appear. "King Oval" was one of these, also "Porlip Oval".

"Man and Beast" remedies had fascinating labels.
Frasier Thornton & Co. were well known in Nova Scotia and Quebec, they also had a branch in Saskatoon.

Right — another "Man and Beast" remedy, but this one could be used internally as well as externally.
Earache and cracked heels hardly seem to require the same medication, but its what the label says. Note the Beaver trade mark.

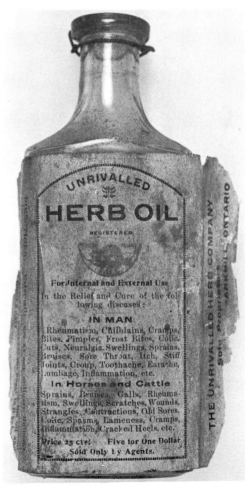

The F. F. Dalley Co., Limited

IT was in the year that Hamilton was incorporated as a city, that the well-known house of F. F. Dalley Co. was established, and that the concern has kept pace with the city in the market of progress and prosperity, must be satisfying to its founders and present heads. The F. F. Dalley company is known from one end of Canada to the other, and also in many other British possessions by its standard goods. Its list of manufactured and prepared products is extremely large and includes baking powders, hygienic self rising flours, flavoring extracts, fruit colorings, starches, ground spices, package drug sundries, mustards, coffees, herbs, bird seeds, butter colors, perfumes, blackings, shoe dressings, stove polishes, harness oil dressings and soaps, oils, inks, mucilage, patent medicines, lyes, tinctures, etc.

The business, of course, was not always so large as it now appears. There was a time in the beginning of things, when but three hands were employed. Today there are fifty hands, not including the fourteen travelers who are all the time on the road looking after the company's varied interests with the wholesale and retail trade of every province in the Dominion. The works of this long established and up-to-date company are located on Hughson street north, quite near the center of the city. Retailers and others visiting the city who may be interested, are always sure of a warm welcome if they desire to see the works.

There is not an inch of waste or spare room in the whole of the immense establishment, all the floor space being needed to store the raw materials and the finished stock before they are shipped.

F. F. Dalley is the president of this most successful company, and E. A. Dalley, a brother, is vice-president. Both the heads of the company are well known men in the public life of the city, being always to the front in enterprises of a public sort and being ever ready to lend a helping hand in any movement calculated to improve the business or social interests of the community. F. F. Dalley for many years represented the citizens on the board of education, being peculiarly well qualified for the position. The secretary-treasurer of the company is R. M. Allworth. The company was incorporated in 1893, and is now doing business with a capital stock of $90,000. Of recent years much attention has been paid to the exporting business and today there is a large trade of an export sort done with Great Britian, Australia, South Africa and United States.

One of the company's leaders in the trade just now, meeting with much favor with the people, is the famous Two in One shoe polish, an article that is as good as its name is unique. Another leader is Hirst's Pain Exterminator.

The factory is fitted out with the most expensive and up-to-date machinery known in in this trade, and the company is ever on the lookout for the new things in machinery which have been proven by test and experience to be good. One of the features of the business is the printing office. Here is a well equipped printery belonging to the establishment, all the labels, wrappers, etc., used are printed. This is but one index of the thoroughness and completeness prevailing throughout the whole factory.

F. F. DALLEY

From the Hamilton Spectator Carnival Souvenir of 1903.

A few of the many bottles used by the F.F. Dalley Co. Ltd.,
and   manufactured   for   them   in   Hamilton,   Ontario.

The cone shaped bottle was popular with other companies
and can be found coast to coast, some like the centre one
still labelled and complete with contents.

Three sizes of pottery ink bottles marked Joseph Bourne & Son, Patentees, Denby Pottery, Near Derby. Tallest bottle, 10 in. high, with original contents and sealed cork.

A selection of early ink bottles. The majority
from the Burlington Glass Works.

Three ink wells.

Ink bottles on display at the Fort Steele Historic Museum, British Columbia.

Photographs on this page show bottles found under floor of barn and in farm dump by Mrs Dennis Campion, Lyndale, P.E.I.

Top photograph — left to right:
Green wine or liquor bottle, 14½ in. high.
Green wine or liquor bottle.
Early Dutch case bottle, embossed as shown.
Deep amber BIMAL.

Centre — left to right:
Dark green bottle, 11½ in. high.
Dark green cup mold bottle.
"Black" liquor bottle with seal.
Deep amber liquor bottle, embossed "Camuslyn Still Registered 170938.

Bottom — left to right:
Dark amber wine or liquor, 12½ in. high.
Whiskey bottle, embossed:
"P. Dawson Distillery"
Black cup mold bottle.
Black cup mold bottle, 10½in.

LOOKING FOR BOTTLES

Digging can yield good results if you have chosen the right place. Haphazard week-end explorations can be time wasting and poking around with a metal detector can be equally frustrating if the spot is wrong.

Bottles are most likely to be found at such places as Century Farms, abandoned homesteads, derelict barns, sites of former glass works, soda water manufactures, early distilleries, old wineries, breweries, old mining operations, county dumps and the warehouses where fruits, sauces, pickles and other foods were packed.

DO NOT TRESPASS, ask permission to seek bottles from the owners or authorities concerned.

The best way to locate the sites mentioned is to check pre-1920 directories, county atlases, plans at the Borough Surveyors office or those of the City Engineer. Your local library may have on hand early directories and other documents relating to local history. It is also a good idea to talk to old timers, as their anecdotes and scraps of information heard in their youth may lead you to a good dig and save hours of searching.

Having decided where to dig make it a group activity, it is easier and more rewarding that way. Choose a nice clear day, pack a picnic and be prepared for hard work. A fork, small spade, wood rake and a trowel should be part of your equipment. You'll need to wear sturdy boots with a practical outfit and don't forget gloves to protect your hands.

There are several likely spots around the old country homes to explore: back of where the outhouse used to be, under the floor boards of the old barn, even the old well is likely to yield treasures.

Where the site of the dump is not evident, head downhill towards where the wall or boundary was. If there are woods across from it, check for signs of a cart track grown over but still likely to be visible. Somewhere around you may notice a depression where the refuse has sogged down, possibly fragments of purpling or yellowing glass and oddments of rusting metal. You may make several tentative starts, but with three or four of you combining your efforts it won't take long before you make a strike.

The old factories or closed out warehouse sites need caution, since rotting stairs and floor boards are hazards, so do the old mining areas since shafts can be concealed by underbrush.

Don't overlook the exploration of streams in the vicinity of works, farms, lumbering or old hunting camps.

As you dig and discover bottles other relics will surface, like sad irons, keys, locks, pots, door knobs, candlesticks and even guns. Think twice before you throw them back, maybe you have a bonus in the form of good swapping material.

Figurals are seldom found in dumps, but do turn up at shows and flea markets as well as in the regular antique stores. This one photographed at:

"Dust and Cobwebs", Stanstead, Quebec.

175

CANADIAN FRUIT JARS

Canadian Fruit Jars have been seen embossed as follows:
1. *ACME with L.G. CO. trade mark.*
2. *BURNS*
3. *COLUMBIAN – MADE IN CANADA.*
4. *One gal. amber – DYSONS PURE FOOD PRODUCTS embossed on base.*
5. *ERIE with AJAX BAKING POWDER embossed on lid.*
6. *MALKINS—AYLMER CANNING CO.*
7. *PURE GOLD MFG CO LTD C.G. Rd. Vase shape,. 3½ in. high.*

The firm of J.W. Sutherland was started in 1897 and is still one of the leading businesses in Hamilton today.

Three years after starting with a small place and one wagon Mr Sutherland doubled the size of his premises and needed four wagons. He imported the highest quality machinery and an expert engineer from England to manage the aerated water works.

J.W. Sutherland manufactured fruit flavoured carbonated waters under the trade names "Crystal Beverages" and "Jamaica Ginger", also many, many, other lines.

Containers used included splits, pints and siphons in a variety of colours.

Aqua bottle, embossed as shown.
Early Holbrook sauce bottle, aqua.

CLEANING BOTTLES

Having found bottles you'll need to clean them. There are several methods, but all the best begin by emptying as much of the muck that has got inside as you possibly can.

Half fill a large vessel with luke-warm suds to which a generous amount of ammonia has been added. Don't put in too many bottles at a time; now leave them for several days.
WARM WATER, NOT HOT OR COLD. Many bottles are lost by being subjected to extreme temperatures.

Rinse bottles and clean by using a spout or baby bottle brush to shift any stuff adhering to the sides. Put in a handful or two of tiny stones or lead shot and swirl them around to take off stubborn stains and polish the inside. Rinse again and clean the outer bottle with a sudsy S.O.S. pad or fine soapy steel wool.

Don't do this in the kitchen sink, a tub or bowl outside is better.

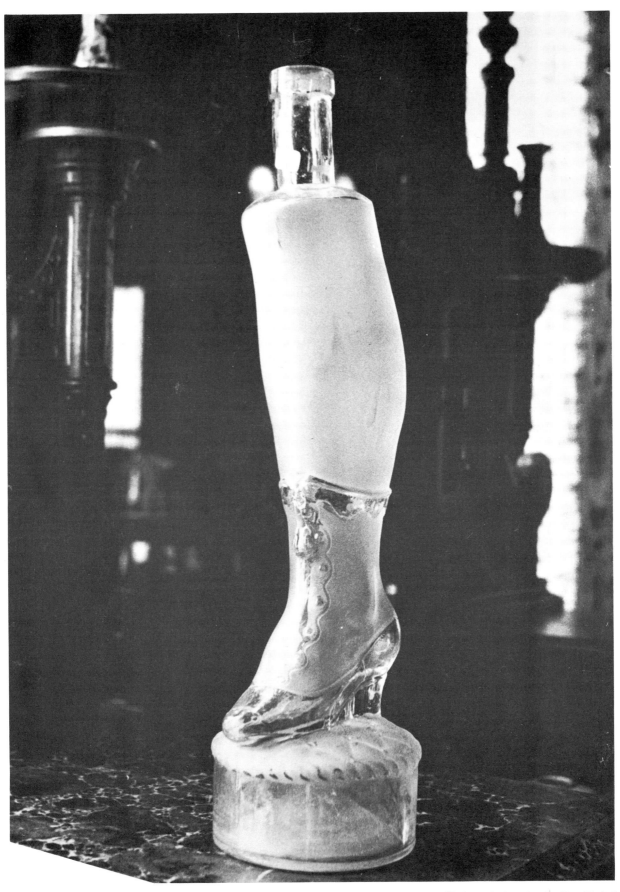

Decorative French bottle, 15 in. high.

FIGURALS

These character or fantasy bottles have been the delight of the gift giver over a very long period. Some of the very best were made between the years 1830 to 1900. As these were special orders and designs created for distilleries, parfumeries. medicine men and others wanting individual bottles they were usually of quality material and workmanship.

When splendour of surroundings was the mark of a good saloon, owners vied with each other in the array of bottles displayed on the shelves. At Christmas they would order the figurals from France and England in pottery and glass and present them to special customers. This created desire in others and a brisk trade in fancy bottles resulted. Since they were available for a short time only they were naturally treasured by the recipient.

The patent medicine makers realised the appeal of the fancy bottle and had their own designs made and before long log cabins, fish, monkeys, barrels, fat men and other containers appeared on drug store shelves.

Public figures were immortalized in the shape of bottles, Queen Victoria, Jenny Lind, Napoleon, Victor Hugo, Robert E. Lee and many, many others.

The Bennington Works produced the coachman and the monk character bottles for a liquor firm and also made a book bottle which held a half gallon.

The variety of design became so wide that it would be hard to list them. Such items as bananas, pretzels, cigars, shoes, hands, violins, turkeys and cooking pots were fashioned by bottle makers and used for products such as liquors, perfumes, bitters, oils, candies, olives, syrups, pickles and sauces. Sizes ranged from a height of 1½ in. to 17 in. The majority of figurals or fancy bottles for liquor came in quart sizes, but some were made to take a half pint and others were small enough to contain a few nips and could be tucked into a pocket or purse without attracting attention to their contents.

Many of these are to be found in Canada since they were imported from France and England as well as from America along with other desirable commodities.

There has been a revival of interest in the fancy bottle for packaging over the past twenty years and some firms have created limited editions of specific designs. Where this has happened the bottles have gained in value even before the supply has run out. There has been a re-issuing of bottles thought to be limited

and this has led to a lowering of price on those put out by cosmetic firms. The liquor companies seem to have definitely limited the numbers made. Certain products are available packed in figurals, such as the Sandeman Port in the Cloaked Cavalier bottle and Buchanan's Black & White Whiskey in the Two Scottie Dog bottles.

Opposite page — Italian cherub bottle,
clear glass. Height 12 in.

Below — Pelican, not original stopper.
Height 18 in. Italian.
Ornamental bottle, 18 in. high. Italian.
Violin, blue, 8 in. high. American.

Cat with bow tie, clear glass, sheared lip.
Height 8½ in. French.

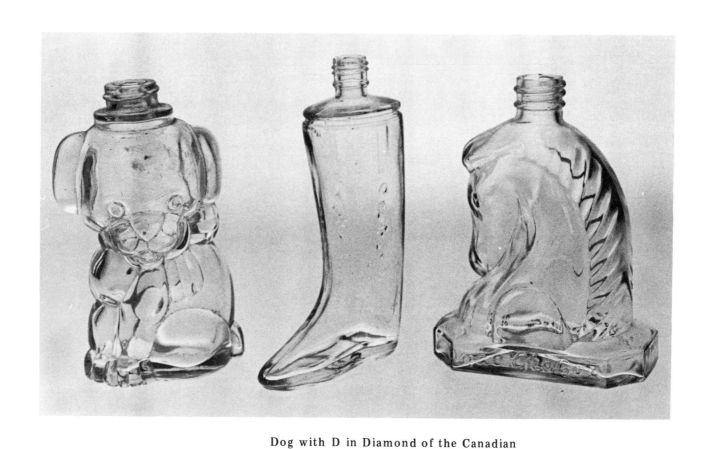

Dog with D in Diamond of the Canadian Dominion Glass Company on the base. Many such animal novelties were made around the late 1930's — 40's period, but are becoming hard to find.

Boot is unmarked — possibly Avon.

Horse is embossed McGregor.

Below — Three perfume bottles, tallest 6½ in.

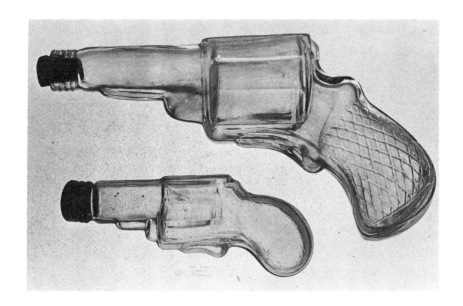

Candy containers come in all shapes and sizes. Revolvers were produced in Canadian factories, also dogs, cats, hats, trains and other novelties.

Below — Old time locomotive, no marks and a Jeep embossed "Patented J.H. Millstein & Co, Jeanette, Pa."

Above — Revolver, fire engine and lace-up shoe.

Contemporary ceramic bottles like these can be found
on the gift counters of department stores across Canada.

Canadian Historic Bottle made to commemorate the incorporation of the Hudson's Bay Company - May 2, 1670.

Rum bottle — full — can be
obtained in L.C.B.O. stores.

Musical novelty bottle, made
in Japan. Gift store item.

HISTORY AND DATA OF CANADIAN SEALERS

(Condensed from NORTH AMERICAN FRUIT JAR INDEX, courtesy Marion & Douglas Bird)

THE ACME SEAL

Made at the Manitoba Glass Manufacturing Company, Beausejour, Manitoba (1907-1914). A shard was found on the site, see Max Provick, **Beausejour's Glass Works,** Canadian (antiques) Collector, January, 1967.

BEAVER

Beaver jars manufactured at the Ontario Glass Company, Kingsville, Ontario (1899-1902). John Sheeler dug up the Beaver pieces at the site. Now at the Canadian Gallery in Toronto. The Beaver Jar was not made by the Beaver Flint Glass Company (Toronto, Ontario, 1897-1948). This firm was a secondary manufacturer, making tubes, vials, etc., from glass tubing supplied by primary manufacturers. The pint size is by far the scarcest.

BEAVER FACING LEFT

Pale aqua pints and amber pints. The ground lip would be of pre-1902 manufacture, and possibly by Dominion's predecessor, Diamond Glass Co. (1890-1902).

CORONA JAR

Made in Canada by Consumers Glass Company. The "C" within an equilateral triange on the bottom is the trademark. Later, the three corners of the triangle were rounded.

THE DOOLITTLE

Manufactured at Wallaceburg, Ontario, by the Sydenham Glass Co. in 1901. It has a very unusual closure, the glass lid carrying two metal "ears", that swing around and hook over the neck. Dominion Glass Company manufactured a jar with a lightening fastener in 1915. It is embossed ERIE-LIGHTENING. Their catalogues show this only in the quart size, the pint and half-gallon sizes being plain. However, there is an earlier ERIE, manufactured at the Erie Glass Works, Port Colborne, Ontario (1895-1899). Not much is known of this firm's output. They made a pickle jar with the word ERIE on the bottom, and a picnic flask with the same marking. Their fruit jars embossed ERIE-E (framed in hexagon) FRUIT JAR. The word ERIE on the bottom, and a ground lip. Its glass lid has a large E in a hexagon.

THE EGCO IMPERIAL

Made by the Excelsior Glass Co. (St. Johns, Quebec 1878-1880; Montreal, Quebec, 1880-1883). It takes a plain glass lid. The Excelsior Glass Company manufactured a glass lid with their name, but color and scarcity indicate that this was for another jar, not yet known.

EXCELSIOR GLASS CO. REGISTERED APR. 1879

Mark on above mentioned lid.

CANADIAN SEALERS

WALLACEBURG
"DOOLITTLE" - Patented Dec. 3, 1901

THE AMERICAN QUART
PORCELAIN LINED

ANCHOR PINT

ANCHOR QUART

EXCELSIOR GLASS CO. INCORPORATED 1879

Since the American firm, EXCELSIOR GLASS WORKS ran from 1863 to 1886, there can be no confusion. The date usually given for the incorporation of EXCELSIOR IN CANADA 1878. However, their lid shows that the actual incorporation went through in 1879.

THE GEM RUTHERFORDS

Made by Hamilton Glass Works during the period of the Rutherford ownership (starting in 1872).

PERFECT SEALS

Made in 1915 by Dominion Glass Company. The STAR is a very rare jar, coming in three sizes, pint, quart and half-gallon. In shape, shape of bottom, mold markings, colour, it exactly resembles the BEAVER. The possibility that it could have been made by Ontario Glass Manufacturing Company is being considered.

CROWNS

Crowns manufactured from 1929 on have the date on the bottom, and are made by Dominion Glass Company. Occasionally the date is missing on the bottom. AQUA CROWNS with smooth lips manufactured 1902 and 1928 inclusive, if there is no date on the bottom. A few of these jars have HD4, HD5, 4DH on the bottom. This means Hamilton Works of the Dominion Glass Company, and it is thought that 4 stands for 1924, and so on, although it has never been established that it does not stand for 1914. CROWN EMBLEM appears on a pint manufactured in 1915 by Dominion. In that year they made a quart and a half gallon with CROWN emblems. (These are shown in one of their catalogues). CROWN EMBLEM appears in a 1924 canning booklet put out by Dominion Glass Co. CROWN EMBLEM also appears in 1902 Eaton's Catalogue. A NEW CROWN EMBLEM (in the heart-shaped series). The half gallon is now known to have been made in 1880. It is very likely that all the heart-shaped crown emblems date about 1880. THE CROWNS with no dots are thought to have been manufactured by Hamilton Glass Works very shortly after 1867. Hamilton started off in 1865 with closures of the type found in the 1861 Millvilles. The no-dot crown is attributed to Hamilton by glass collectors because the mold-markings, the shape of the jar, and the base shape exactly resemble the GEM RUTHER FORDS, which are known to have been made at Hamilton. It is thought that the crown emblem was originally used on pottery to indicate Imperial measure.

THE DEXTER

The Dexter has a mouth part-way between a small-mouth pint, and a regular pint, exactly resembling the mouth of the certain GEM RUTHERFORDS, and would therefore be of Hamilton manufacture. (Geo. Rutherford and Company were the owners of Hamilton Glass Works in 1872. From 1865 to 1871, Gachell, Moore and Company were the owners.)

GEM

GEM (script), NEW GEM (script), 1908, GEM (script), Wallaceburg, GEM (script) are so very similar in design and glass that they can all be attributed to the Wallaceburg plant of Sydenham Glass Co. (later the Dominion Glass Co., Wallaceburg plant).

THE GREEK KEY DESIGN JAR

Manufactured by Burlington Glass Co. See Royal Ontario Museum leaflet.

CANADIAN SEALERS

BEAVER Crosshatch Tail
American one-half gallon

AMBER BEAVER
facing left (rare)

BEAVER Stipple tail
Imperial one-half gallon

BEE HIVE
One-half gallon

BEST
One quart

THE BURLINGTON
B.G. Co. Quart
Note mismarked B.C. Go.

CANADIAN SEALERS

BURLINGTON QUART
1880

CORONET
One half gallon

CROWN
No Dot

RING WITH CROWN
No Word - gallon

CROWN
Word on - one half gallon

CROWN
Bulge quart

189

CANADIAN SEALERS

CROWN
Tall, Narrow

DEXTER
Quart

DIAMOND
D.G. Co., One-half gallon

THE GEM
Rutherford & Co.
Hamilton Glass Co.

THE SAME
Embossing Different

GEM
H.F.C. on Wings of Cross

CANADIAN SEALERS

IDEAL IMPERIAL
Quart

HAMILTON GLASSWORKS
One quart

HAMILTON GLASSWORKS
No. 2

HAMILTON GLASSWORKS
No. 4
Has whittle marks
due to cold mould

HAMILTON GLASSWORKS
One-half gallon

STAR
One quart

CANADIAN SEALERS

THE EGGO
Imperial Quart

THE ROSE

TRUE FRUIT
J. H. S. Co.

GREEK KEY
One-half gallon

THE POINTS TO NOTE
WHEN COLLECTING SEALERS

FACTOR	POSITIVE QUALITIES	NEGATIVE QUALITIES
Embossing	prominent and distinct	worn looking
Closure	Complete, proper, matching closure	No closure, Incorrect closure, Partial closure
Condition	No damage	Lip chips, cracks in lip, stain
Color	Attractive color	Less attractive
Glass	Whittled, bubbly	Machine-like
Metal closure	Old but no damage	Rusty, corroded
Screw band	Tightens properly	Threads stripped

See Bird, North American Fruit Jar Index

Amber Beaver — facing right
Ontario Glass Co. 1899 — 1902

Aqua Beaver — facing right,
poor imprint.

Best, rayed base.   Diamond
Flint or Dominion Glass Co.

Corona Jar, made from 1917 to
1950 by Consumers Glass Co.

Corona Jar, made from 1917 to
now by Consumers Glass Co.

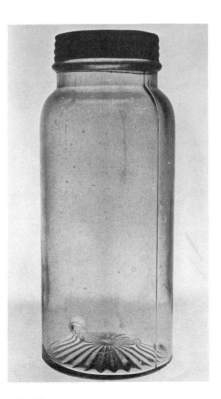

5 lb. Candy Jar. Dominion
Glass Co. Catalogue Nos. 8 & 9.

Hamilton Glass Works product.

Mason jar, 1913 — 1928.
Note reverse "N".

Mid-West Glass Co, Winnipeg,
Manitoba, 1929 — 1931.

The "Perfect Seal" with vines,
circa 1915.

"Perfect Seal", ht. 6½ in. suncast amethyst. c.1913—1914.

"Perfect Seal", in shield. Ordinary type. c.1915.

Photograph supplied by John MacDonald.

Improved Jam — Lamont Glass Co. (1890—1898). Height 9 in. Applied neck and ground top.

The Darling has never been definitely traced to any factory or firm. Julian Toulouse considers it possibly Canadian. It is shown in the "Century of Canadian Fruit Jars" with the comment "maker not known. The meaning of the ADM (order of letters not known)".

Handsome 4 lb. pear-shaped candy. by Whitall & Tatum Co., U.S.A. Canadian jars of this type usually have rayed base.

Photograph supplied by John MacDonald.

Food jars, various shades of aqua. All with applied necks.   Tallest — second from left — 9½ in.

Photograph supplied by John MacDonald.

Dominion Pattern   4 lb. square candy.

Three pickle jars — Diamond or Dominion Glass Company (1895 — 1925).

Rare quart Crown sealer, no cross.

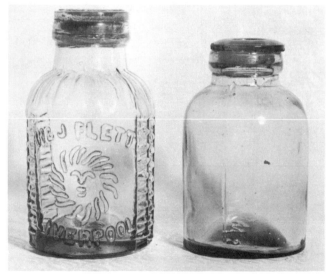

Photograph supplied by John MacDonald.

Above — two aqua jars with applied necks, glass lids and cork liners. Taller jar 7½ in. Right hand jar embossed "W & W double refined salt". Date of these jars c. 1880.

Right — Skunk Cabbage — obviously had some medicinal value, but how it was prepared or taken could not be ascertained. Description in the Encyclopedia Britannica: "A fleshy herbaceous plant of the Arum family (Araceae), so called because of its fetid odour and large leaves. Native to North America and North Eastern Asia.

Two Dominion Glass Co. jars, made for McLarens, Hamilton.

Left — embossed on base: McLarens Ltd., Hamilton, Canada, and the D in Diamond trade mark of Dominion Glass.

Right — embossed on base: McLarens, Hamilton — design registered and the D in Diamond trade mark.

Below —
16 oz. "Bambino Olive" jar, reusable as piggy bank. Lid made in U.S.A. Embossed on base: Gattuso Corpn., Montreal, also the D in Diamond trade mark.

Left —
Interesting mustard jar with applied lip.

The "cream top" came into vogue during the early 1920's as a result of 'cream content' being a selling point with the dairies. Since this style is less plentiful than others it is of more value to collectors. Milk bottles were first used commercially in the Americas about 1884. Dr Thatcher of New York is credited with designing the first glass milk bottles. He made pint and quart sizes and had an embossed picture of a cow being milked by a man and the words "Absolutely Pure Milk — The Milk Protector".

Baby bottles or "nursers" as they are listed in early catalogues date back a long time and were made in many styles and sizes. The first American glass nurser was patented 1841 by Charles M. Windship. A variety of nursing bottles are shown in the Dominion Glass Company catalogues of the early 1900's. Bottle shown below with long rubber tube originated c. 1864.

Two Canadian nursers from Dominion Glass Company.

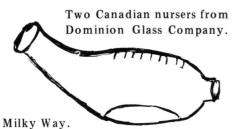

Milky Way.

Excelsior.

Below —
Two nursers from the Mac Provick collection.

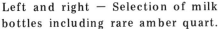
Left and right — Selection of milk bottles including rare amber quart.

DAIRY BOTTLES

Bottle collecting was at one time confined to the collecting of figurals, perfumes and snuff bottles. It then spread to include early wine and liquor bottles. Now the collector's choice has widened and old drug bottles, fruit jars, sauce bottles, beer bottles, soda pops, stone gingers, ink bottles, in fact any and every shape that can be termed a bottle including the humble milk bottle forms a part of his display.

The round milk bottle started to disappear from our doorsteps and dairy shelves around 1947-8 when somebody bright realised that a bottle fashioned after our old friend the case bottle would actually carry better, pack better and fit on madam's refrigerator shelf more easily and save space.

The attractive thing about the dairy bottle is that it came in various patterns and different sizes. Almost all were embossed with the names and trade marks of the dairies which used them, some very elaborately. Some firms had specially designed bottles which depicted a cow or cow with milk maid, or other designs such as animals, birds, stars and babys. From around 1935 applied colour labelling was used and the quart bottle on Page IV is an excellent example of this art.

By 1957 the round milk bottle was made for only a few dairies in the Maritimes and Quebec, this type of bottle is now considered a desirable collectable. Since most of these are trade marked by either Doninion or Consumer's Glass there is no doubt as to their Canadian origin. The majority of milk bottles are of clear glass, but an amber bottle was offered by the Dominion Glass Company, catalogue No. 15 (c. 1910), and put into use by some dairies.

When you check a collection of round milk or cream bottles you will find that many names have vanished, since large combines absorbed smaller firms. See Page 201.

199

Collecting milk bottles is a
fascinating pursuit for several
reasons. One being that they
are still around. Two that they
are within the reach of the collector of modest means. Three:
facts may be readily gathered
from local directories and lastly
since there is a wide assortment
of sizes and styles to add interest it can cover a span of several
years to get a representative
collection   together.   Most

Several shapes and sizes of
dairy bottles are shown on this
page. Left — Note the small
individual creamers.
Above — Half pint, pint and
quart sizes.
Below — Earlier bottles with
lightening stoppers.

dairies had from three to eight
sizes, some had amber bottles
for buttermilk.   There were
special shapes for chocolate
milk, very small bottles for use
in restaurants, a little larger
size for the serving of cream
and others to contain anything
from 1 gill to ½ gallon of milk.
Tops included a lightening type
stopper, cardboard disks, corks
and later foil caps.

200

FACTS ABOUT DAIRIES

The Dairy Corporation of Canada, incorporated 1929, owned the following dairies as of December 31st, 1931:

City Dairy Ltd., Winnipeg, Man.
The Davis Dairy Ltd., Saskatoon, Sask.
Edmonton Dairy Ltd., Edmonton, Alta.
Montreal Dairy Co., Montreal, Que.
The Prairie Creameries, Regina, Sask.
The Purity Dairy Ltd., Regina, Sask.
Purity Ice Cream Co., Winnipeg, Man.
Canada Dairies Ltd., Toronto, Ont.

They also had substantial interests in other dairy companies in Canada.

The Farmer's Dairy, the Acme Dairy Ltd. and Moore's Model Dairy amalgamated in 1929 and the business operated as Acme Farmer's Dairy Ltd.

The Borden Company was established in 1857 in New Jersey, U.S.A.

The Canadian Company, Borden's Ltd., was incorporated December 2nd, 1930 and acquired control of the following:

Ballantyne Windsor City Dairy Ltd.
Canadian Milk Products Ltd.
Caulfield's Dairy Ltd., Toronto, Ont.
Chateau Cheese Co., Ltd., Ottawa, Ont.
City Dairy Co., Ltd., Toronto, Ont.
Cornwall Dairy Products Ltd., Ont.
The Drimilk Co., Ltd., Toronto, Ont.
Halls Ltd., Toronto & Winnipeg.
Hamilton Dairies Ltd.
J.J. Joubert Ltee., Montreal, Que.
Moyneue Co-operative Creamery,
Ottawa Dairy, Ltd.   Ottawa.
Pure Milk Co., Ltd., Hamilton, Ont.
Walkerside Dairy Ltd., Walkerville, Ont.

Photograph taken at the Nova Scotia Museum.

Robert Turlington
"Balsam of Life" bottle.

Robert Turlington is credited with being the first manufacturer of patent medicine to use embossed bottles. The famous "Balsam of Life" was patented in 1744. To protect the buyers from imitations Turlington decided to package his medication in this very distinctive bottle.

His patent listed 27 ingredients and when the supply to the Americas from London, England, was cut off during the War of Independence not only did the druggists make up their own version of the balsam, but had the bottles copied. Therefore several variations of the medication were on the market at the same time, the bottles also having differences of size and colour.

In 1833 the various compounds being sold as Turlington's were analysed by the Philadelphia College of Pharmacy and their findings were that it was doubtful that Turlington's own product any longer contained exactly what had been listed in the original patent. After the investigation the Pharmacists created a formula based on Turlington's Balsam of Life and it was later standardised as Compound Tincture of Benzoin.

Some years ago the trade name Friars Balsam was added and that is how it is marketed today.

The original Turlington bottle is highly collectable and even the variations command a high price. The complete inscription reads: front — "BY THE KING'S ROYAL PATENT GRANTED TO and back — ROBT TURLINGTON FOR HIS INVENTED BALSAM OF LIFE", on one side the word LONDON and on the other the date JAN 26, 1756.

"Friars Balsam" is packaged today in a **regular** patent medicine bottle.

PICTURE BOTTLES

An interesting collection can be made of what might be termed Picture Bottles. This is a diverting category since it includes any bottle embossed with a picture as well as words and includes:
Early London Winery Ltd. bottles.
Mineral water bottles with beavers, birds, squirrels etc.
Medicinals with apothecary's scales or pestle and mortar.
Beer bottles with wheatsheafs, beavers and many other emblems.
Jumbo bottles, mammy bottles, bottles with peppers and gherkins pictured as a still life.
Dairy bottles with babies, cows and milkmaids etc.
Then there are the monkeys, cherubs, barrels, wine presses, lighthouses, skeletons, bugs, flies, old father time and the bottles with the portraits of famous personalities.
Warner's Safe Cure is almost a category on its own. This bottle has an embossing of a safe on the front, but the cure was sold in many countries and bottles are embossed with various place names, i.e. Toronto, Canada; London, England; Melbourne, Australia; Rochester, N.Y.

Blue Italian bottle, embossed with sailing ship.

Above — left to right:
Shell Motor Oil bottle. 1933 and D in Diamond mark embossed on bottom.   Height 15½ in.

Mammy Beverages Co. bottle. D in Diamond mark. Height 14 in.

Jumbo Beverages Co. bottle. D in Diamond mark. Height 14 in.

London Winery Ltd. bottle. Embossed with man at wine press and D in Diamond on base.

Left — English Victoria Diamond Jubilee bottle, embossed with hands holding glasses. Ht. 4½ in.

Below right — Sutherland bottle, embossed as shown. Height 5 in.

Left — two embossed bottles.
Warner's Safe Cure bottle embossed:
"London, England" & "Rochester, N.Y."
Right — Rumming's bottle, with internal thread, embossed with pick and shovel design.

Below right — O.T. Ltd. sauce bottle with still life of peppers embossed. This is another bottle of many countries, having been produced in England, Canada and Australia. The Canadian version was made by Dominion Glass Co., Montreal. O.T. is an abreviation of Old Time.

Below left — two sizes Midland Vinegar Company bottles, embossed as shown.

Three Stower's Lime Juice Cordial bottles. Advertised — "as supplied to Her Most Gracious Majesty The Queen". Distributor A. Riddell & Co., London, England. Deep aqua-blue. Heavily embossed. Smallest 10 in. high.

Maple leaf bottle, as shown in Dominion Catalogues Nos. 8 and 9.

Rose's Lime Juice bottle. Aqua. B.I.M., applied lip. Height 14 in.

Orange de Luxe, 7½ in. high. A.B.M., crown cap. D in Diamond mark.

Perfume bottles as shown in the 1888 catalogue of the Toronto Silver Plate Company.

No. 0801—TOILET SET.
$20.00 (*Juicy*)

No. 0800—TOILET SET.

Plain, - - - - - $19.00 (*Journal*)
Gold Inlaid, - - - - 22.00 (*Journey*)

No. 903—COLOGNE STAND.

Blue or Amber Glass, Richly Decorated.

$6.50   (*Juggler*)

No. 923—COLOGNE STAND.

Rose or Blue Glass.

Gold Decoration,   - $6.25   (*Shade*)

No. 922—COLOGNE STAND.

Plain Silver,   -   - $5.50   (*Junction*)

No. 924—COLOGNE STAND.

Rose or Blue Glass.

Gold Decoration,   -   - $6.00   (*Shaft*)

Two contemporary whiskey bottles.
Left — Brown and cream.
Right — Jim Beam, blue ceramic.

Above — Green glazed pottery bottle.
Canadian made. Signed M.G. 58.
Height 15 in.

Left — Blue and white glass
lamp shape perfume bottle.
Height 5¾ in.

Pair of decanters trimmed with silver
plated grape vines.   Height 9½ in.

Ceramic Maple Leaf
bottle. Height 4 in.

Three sizes of liquor flasks,
curved to fit the pocket.

Chestnut bottle with
applied lip. Ht. 10 in.

Bottle with leather carrying case, possibly military. Rubber stopper with metal core.

Nineteenth century bottle, still in original basket-work container.

Shoulder flask in woven carry-case.

English hot water bottle. Many of these were sold in Canada.

Powder flasks from the collection of Allan and Vera Fraser,
Lamplighter Antiques, Pike Bay, Ont.

Two pressed glass cruets and a syrup jug in Westmoreland Block pattern. These are a specialized field of collecting like perfume and snuff bottles, however there are very beautiful examples in these groups to be found in Canada. The above are from the collection of Mr and Mrs J. Welbourne, Peterborough, Ontario.

Three lovely and desirable cruets. Left to right — Caramel slag, amber with blue stopper and handle, peach blow with amber handle. Collection of Mr and Mrs Garnet Hazard, Fallbrook, Ont.

Left —
Sanctuary lights. Clear on left, orange on right. These were also made in red and blue. Base of light on right embossed: "F. Baillargeon" and "Made in U.S.A."

Right — Small Holy Water bottle. It should stand on a small glass plate and have a stopper.

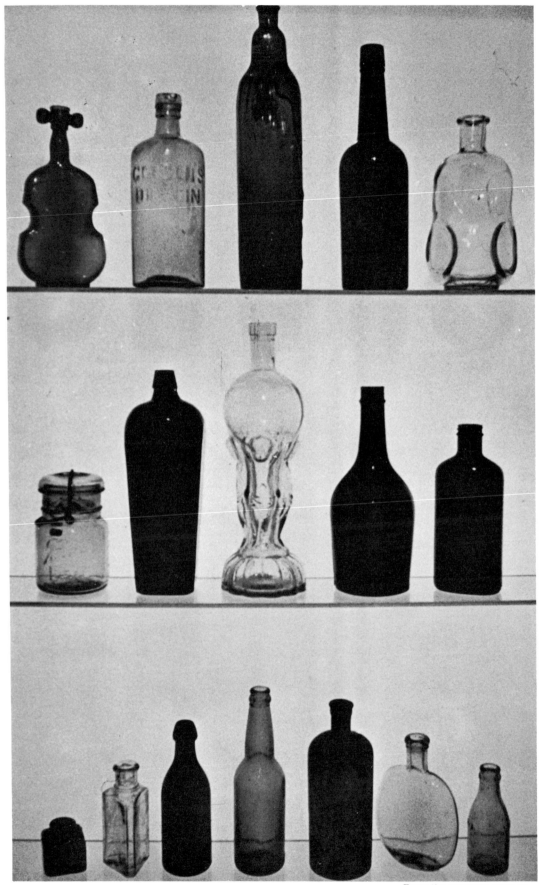

Glass shelves are excellent for the display of bottles.

PRICING ISN'T EASY

Pricing is one of the aspects of collecting that requires a great deal of consideration and restraint. If you are a 'digger' you will have spent many hours locating suitable digs, then in the digging and later in sorting and cleaning your finds.

Now you are wondering and endeavouring to get an idea of the value, financial that is, of what you have. Certain types of bottle have already found a price level, but as in all other collectables the levels vary from area to area and dealer to dealer.

One factor to consider is demand. If you know of no other collector in your area and are without outside contacts you will have little or no market for your surplus bottles. On the other hand if you are in touch with other collectors you will be able to swap or sell your spares.

Approximate values can be arrived at but no firm prices can be established on objects that are as yet in limbo. i.e. Canadian bottles are a comparatively new collectable and as such no real appraisal of supply and demand obtains. What can be dug for free cannot be priced fairly until diggings are completed or at least on the point of running out.

The "one of a kind" bottle could suddenly become the "one of many" overnight as more and more collectors start to explore the old dumps or a bottle club excavates an early brewery, distillery or soda water manufactory site.

The following cross-section of prices gives an indication of current values.

SCALE OF VALUES

Extremely Rare, 1 to 5 specimens
known . . . . name your own price.

Rare, 5 to 25, from 100.00

Very scarce, 25 to 100, from 75.00

Scarce, 100 to 500, from 15.00

Plentiful, 500 to 1,000, from 3.00

Commonplace, over 1,000, from 50

A pontil mark is of great importance in dating a a bottle.

Amber or brown fruit jars are worth more than those which are suncast amethyst.

A whittle or chip marked bottle has more value than one of the same type unmarked.

CANADIAN BITTERS BOTTLES:

There were quite a number of Canadian made bitters, Burdock's Blood Bitters being the best known.

Any Canadian bitters bottle, BIM, embossed with name 10.00

Burdock's Blood Bitters, Canadian. . . 12.00

John Bull Bitters, green case bottle, label reads: Meagher Bros & Co., Montreal, Established 1837 . . . . 25.00

Gate's "Life of Man" Bitters, rectangular aqua bottle 18.00

Fellow's Nervine Bitters, labelled and embossed 14.00

CANADIAN MEDICINALS:

For plentiful pre-1900 embossed BIM bottles, such as Minard's and Fellows 3.00

Most prescription bottles 1.50

Canadian Pain Killer, aqua, 1 pint. . . 15.00

The Great Shoshonees Remedy of Dr Josephus, aqua, 1 pint. 25.00

Canadian Cod Liver Oils, BIM, for example — Puttner's, N.S. 12.00

Labelled and embossed medicinals, pre-1900 . . . . 4.00

Man & Beast Remedies, pre-1900. . . . 6.00

Cobalt blue bottles of the Como — Hudson type 20.00

Cobalt blue poison, pre-1913, BIM, according to rarity, from 4.50

Sealed Prescription bottle with contents and original wrapper 18.00

Light green Campbell & Co. medicine bottle 35.00

Large light green Campbell's Elixir . 26.00

Large dark blue BIM medicine bottle. . . 60.00

Blue bottle with monogram on base. . . 40.00

Beauty is of great importance when putting a price on a bottle.

Bubbles in the glass are an indication of age.

Common or utilitarian bottles made after 1860 do not have pontil marks.

BLACK BOTTLES:

Eighteenth century bottles of French, British or Spanish origin.

Free blown, applied lip, black, from. . 75.00

Canadian made bottles from 1840 - 1875.

Free blown, applied lip, black, from. . 100.00

BIMAL, ragged pontil mark, from. . 45.00

BIMAL, bare iron pontil mark, from. . 20.00

BREWERY BOTTLES:

Beer bottles, embossed with brewery name etc., dark olive green, Canadian made 1875 — 1900. Some breweries had more than one variety of embossment. Value depends on rarity here: the shorter the life of the brewery the rarer the bottle.

BIM, from 32.00

Beer bottles as above, but red, from. . . 50.00

Bottles complete with labels as well as being embossed have higher values.

Machine made beer bottles have very varying values according to the length of time the brewery was in business, background facts and the time span of the particular label.

Pre-1913 Canadian made bottles,
from. . . 12.00

Dirty bottles are not always old bottles. If a bottle has been kept in a dry atmosphere it will appear like new even though it is a hundred years old.

Dirty bottles have less value than clean ones.

Bottles with embossed misprints have rarity value.

Historical flasks were whiskey not patent medicine bottles.

Wine bottles made during the eighteenth century were 'black' not aqua in colour.

CANADIAN INKS AND MUCILAGE BOTTLES:

Cone shape, clear, all sizes, from. . . . 3.00

Cone shape, coloured, small, from. . . . 6.00

Square, clear, all sizes, from 1.50

Square, blue, all sizes, from 3.00

Shear tops, from 5.00

All bottles with Canadian labels in the above categories are worth double these prices.

CANADIAN CASE BOTTLES:

Blown in mold (BIM) bottles, from. . . 20.00

CANADIAN MINERAL WATERS:

These bottles range from the rare early torpedo bottles, which become almost priceless when coupled with names like Glendenning, Pilgrim and Bilton to the bottles made by automatic machine in the plentiful group.

Plentiful ABM bottles, from. 75

Early aqua, BIM, rounded base embossed name & trade mark, from. . . 45.00

Early aqua, BIM, flat base, embossed name and trade mark, from . . . 30.00

STONE GINGER BEERS:

Stone ginger beers with Canadian potter's mark 25.00

Stone ginger beers with mark other than Canadian 10.00

Stone ginger beers, no mark, but labelled 10.00

Larger sizes in the above category are worth more according to rarity.

CANADIAN POTTERY JUGS:

Pottery jugs have been seen in all sizes and at a wide range of prices, but those of proven Canadian origin are the most desirable.

Their prices range from. . . . 15.00 to 100.00

POISON!

Photograph taken at Fort Steele Historic Museum.

This was the message of the colour or shape of the bottle. Colour readily identified the dangerous bottles in daylight, particularly for children and anyone unable to read. The square, triangular, or odd-shaped bottles, perhaps with notched edges, could guide hands searching for medicine in darkness or the dead of night.

INSULATORS IN CANADA

Photograph taken at Fort Steele Historical Museum

Insulators were made in many Canadian glass works and have become popular with some glass collectors. The subject is of sufficient interest to require much more research than we have done at this time. Shown are photographs of the types that can be found also drawings from a Dominion Glass Company catalogue published after 1913.

No. 1671 — Standard Telegraph Insulator. Weight average 17 oz. Embossed C.N.R. or C.P.R. Standard or Canadian Pacific Railway Co. or Standard or Montreal Telegraph Co. Colours — aqua-blue, light blue, aqua-green, off-white, deep amethyst. Single petticoat.

POTTERY INSULATORS

White pottery insulators were used by:

C.P.R. Canadian Pacific Railway.

G.T.P. ... Grand Trunk Pacific.

These were so marked with lettering under glaze.

Several other colours in pottery insulators are also found:

Bennington brown, chocolate brown, blue-white, red, light and dark blue.

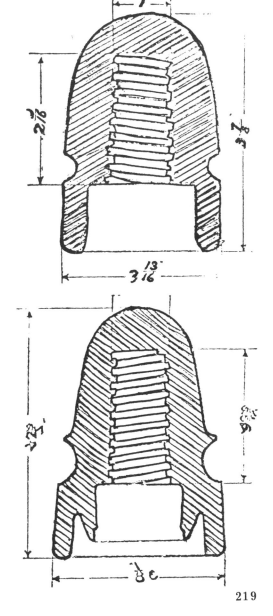

No. 1678 — Extra Deep Groove Double Petticoat. Weight average 19 oz. Embossed 1678 Hamilton Glass Co. Colours — aqua-blue, pale green, suncast yellow, deep amethyst. Two types — with and without drip points.

Photograph taken on railway line between Kaladar and Ottawa, Ontario.

Canadian insulators are fetching good prices, especially the coloured specimens. If you are around when the lines are being changed over you can add some to your collection.

EMBOSSING ON INSULATORS
TO BE FOUND IN CANADA

ARMOURLIGHT	Trade name of Pilkington Glass Co.
B.C.DRIP	Aqua, 3¾ in. high, 3 in. wide, sharp drip points, double petticoat.
B.T.C. CANADA	Bell Telephone Co.
B.T.Co OF CANADA	Bell Telephone Co.
B.T.C. MONTREAL	Bell Telephone Co.
C.N.R.	Canadian National Railway.
C.P.R.	Canadian Pacific Railway.
C.P.R. STANDARD	Canadian Pacific Railway.
STANDARD	Canadian Pacific Railway.
DWIGHT PATTERN	Aqua, 3½ in. high, 2 in. wide, single petticoat.
FOSTER BROS. StJOHN C.E. 1858	'Black', which is actually very dense green-yellow 3¾ in. high, 3½ in. wide.
G.N.W. TEL. CO.	Great North Western Telegraph Co.
G.T.P. TEL. Co.	Canadian made for Grand Trunk Pacific Telegraph Co.
G.T.P. B.	Made by Brookfield Co., America for Grand Trunk Pacific Telegraph.
HAMILTON GLASS CO.	Product of the Hamilton Glass Co.

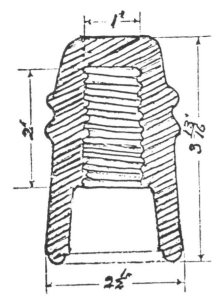

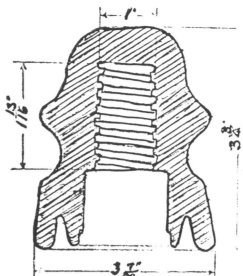

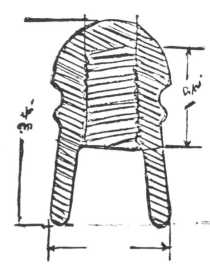

Standard Telephone
Insulator
Weight average 14 oz.
Embossed B.T.C. over
Canada or with two
Diamonds.
Colours — aqua-green,
pale blue, deep amethyst,
Single petticoat.

No. 614. — Extra Deep
Groove, Double Petticoat.
Weight average 18 oz.
Embossed Dominion 614
with D in Diamond or
with Diamond.
Colours — aqua-green,
clear, suncast yellow,
deep amethyst.
Two types — with and
without drip points.

No. 9 — Pony Insulator.
Weight average 9½ oz.
Embossed single large Diamond or two large Diamonds
or two large Diamonds with
"I" above each or "I" on each
half mold, or B.T.C. Canada
or B.T.C. Montreal.
All colours including "black",
which is a very dense yellow-
green. Single petticoat.

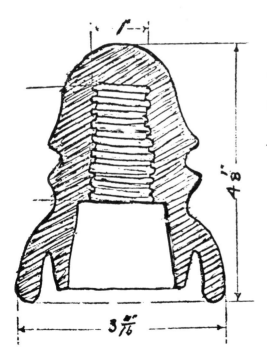

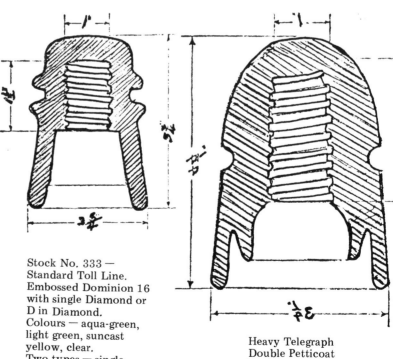

No. 613 — New Western
Union Standard Telegraph.
Double petticoat Insulator.
Weight average 22 oz.
Embossed one Diamond.
Colour — aqua-blue.

Stock No. 333 —
Standard Toll Line.
Embossed Dominion 16
with single Diamond or
D in Diamond.
Colours — aqua-green,
light green, suncast
yellow, clear.
Two types — single
petticoat & without
drip points.

Heavy Telegraph
Double Petticoat
Insulator.
Weight average 25 oz.
Embossed G.N.W. Tel Co.
or G.T.P. Tel Co. or
T.C.R. or T.N.R.
Colours aqua-blue, aqua-
green, suncast yellow.

Bill Hart collection.

Canadian insulators, all shapes, colours and sizes, together with coloured globes used on old time lightening conductors.

Embossing on Insulators contd.

McMICKING VICTORIA B.C. 75	Aqua, small square top insulator, no threads. 3¼ in. high, base 25/16 in.
M.T.C.	Montreal Telegraph Company.
M.T.	Montreal Telegraph Company.
MONTREAL TELEGRAPH CO.	Ditto.
N.W. & B.I.T. CO.	New Westminster & Burrard Inlet Telegraph Co.
PETTICOAT	Maker unknown.
1673	Maker unknown.
GISBORNE PATTERN	White pottery insulator.
DOMINION GLASS COMPANY	Description and pattern drawings in text.

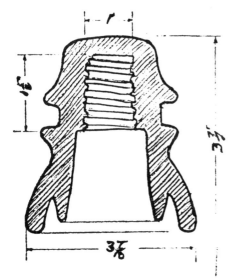

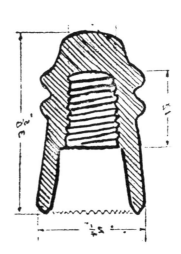

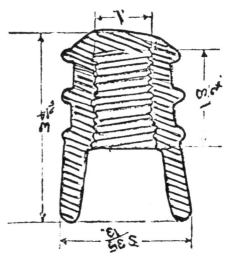

Stock No. 365 — New Heavy.
Telegraph (C.N.T. Style).
Weight average 22 oz.
Embossed Dominion 42 or
Dominion 42 with D in
Diamond.
Colour — aqua-green,
suncast yellow, clear.
Blunt or no drip points.
Double petticoat.

Stock No. 334 —
Special Pony Drip.
Weight average 10 oz.
Embossed Dominion 9
with single squared Diamond
Diamond or Dominion 9
with D in Diamond.
Colours — aqua-green,
clear.
Blunt drip points.
Single petticoat.

Double Groove Insulator.
Weight average 9¾ oz.
Embossed two Diamonds
or Dominion 10 with single
Diamond or Dominion 10
with D in Diamond.
Colours — aqua-green,
suncast yellow, clear.
Two types — one with
& one without drip points.
Single petticoat.

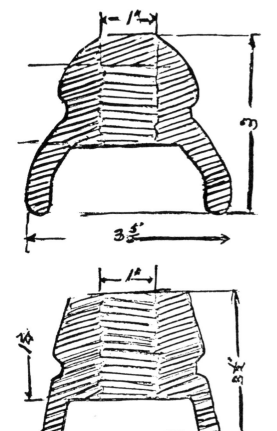

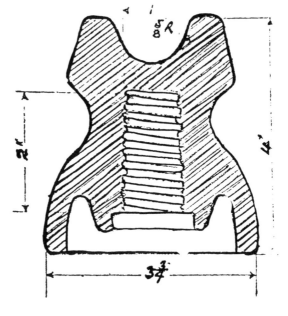

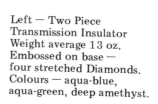

Left — Two Piece
Transmission Insulator
Weight average 13 oz.
Embossed on base —
four stretched Diamonds.
Colours — aqua-blue,
aqua-green, deep amethyst.

Above — No. 2 Cable
Insulator.
Weight average 26 oz.
Embossed —
No. 2 Cable.
Colours — aqua-green,
emerald green.
Rare.

223

"GO—WITHS"

Canadian sterling silver decanter labels on display at the Nova Scotia Museum, Halifax.

Many things "go-with" a bottle collection — trade mugs, advertisements, posters, silver decanter labels, display items, etc. etc.

Below —
Advertising figure
for bar or counter.

Magnum size display bottle.

Scotch Whiskey Jug

Below — Copy of a letter which led us to a gold mine of information. Hamilton, Ontario.
We have many almanacs in our library, usually acquired very slowly. November 4th, 1971.

Peter and Doris Unitt,
P.O. Box 103,
Peterborough, Ontario.

Dear Mr. & Mrs. Unitt:

Your notice in the October 25th issue of Ontario Showcase started me
on a "clean-up" of my book cases. Here is a list of Almanacs in which you
may be interested.

Title	Year	Condition
Toronto Almanac & Canada Calendar	1843	Good – corners worn
Eltons Comic All-My-Nack	1844	Good – corners worn
Canadian Mercantile Almanac	1846	Good – corners worn
Peoples Almanac	1848	Fair .. cover missing
Canadian Mercantile Almanac	1849	Very Good
Scobies Canadian Almanac	1851	Good .. some indication of "mouse" chewing
Almanac	1852	Cover and first page missing
Illustrated Family Christian Almanac	1856	Good
Canadian Almanac	1860	Good .. corners worn
Canadian Almanac	1862	Good
Canadian Almanac	1863	Good
Canadian Almanac	1864	Fair -- cover page missing
Canadian Almanac	1865	Good
The Spectator farmers almanac	1865	Good
Spectator farmers almanac	1866	Good
Canadian almanac	1867	Fair – cover and first few pages show indications of hungry mice
Spectator almanac	1867	Good
Spectator Almanac	1868	Good
Spectator almanac	1870	Good
Rankins Illustrated Almanac	1874	Fair .. the mice got to one corner
Vennors Almanac	1880-81	Good – covering missing
American Agriculturist almanac (size approx 6 x 9 -- 1 inch thick)	1897	excellent
Drug Store? almanac	1857	Poor some front pages missing
Hagetinis almanac (size 1¼" x 2" condition very good)	1894	Condition very good

I don't know what other information I can give you; and have not attempted to
put a present day value on them. If these are of interest to you, please
let me know.

R. J. Burgess

GLASS MANUFACTURE.

Fig. 2. PLATE I.

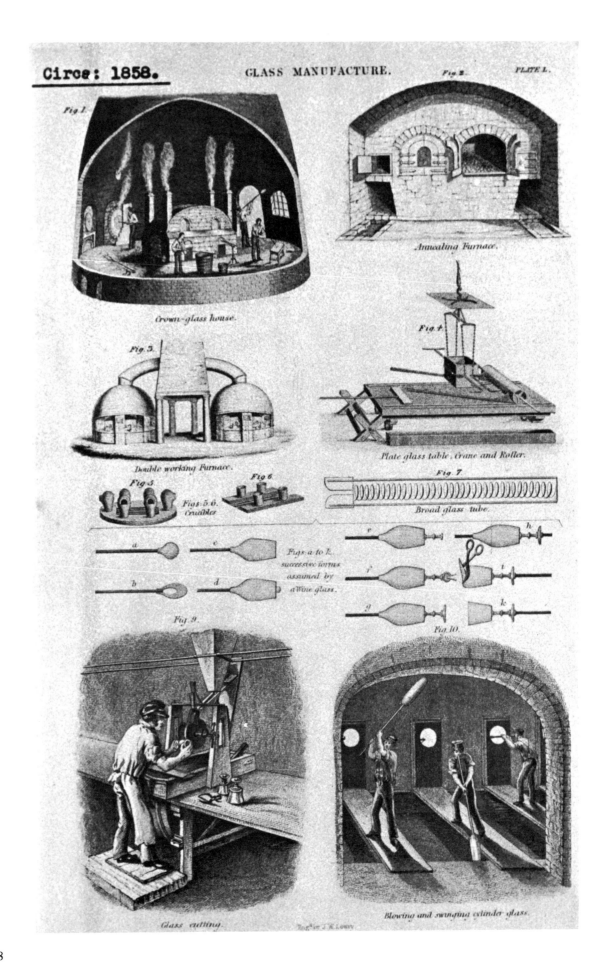

Fig. I.

Crown-glass house.

Annealing Furnace.

Fig. 3.

Double working Furnace.

Fig. 4.

Plate glass table, Crane and Roller.

Fig. 5. *Fig. 6.*

Figs: 5. 6.
Crucibles.

Fig. 7.

Broad glass tube.

a *c*

b *d*

*Figs: a to k.
successive forms
assumed by
a Wine glass.*

e *h*

f *i*

g *k*

Fig. 9. *Fig. 10.*

Glass cutting.

Blowing and swinging cylinder glass.

Eng.d in J. K. Lowry

GLOSSARY

ANNEALING:
The tempering by gradual cooling of hot glassware in the lehr (leer). Initial temperature 950 degrees F.

BATCH:
Raw materials ready for melting in a furnace; melted ingredients ready for blowing, pressing, etc. Temperature for melting 2200 degrees F.

COLOUR:
Glass is by nature seldom free from colour, traces of iron in the sand produces a greenish tone.
GREEN:
Produced by adding iron.
RUBY RED & TURQUOISE BLUE:
Produced by adding copper
BLUE:
Produced by adding colbalt.
AMETHYST, PINK OR PURPLE:
Produced by varying amounts of maganese.
REDS & PINKS:
Produced by varying amounts of gold.
MILK WHITE (dense opaque):
Produced by varying amounts of oxide of tin.
MILK & WATER (semi-opaque and opalescent):
Produced by varying amounts of arsenic compound or calcined bone.

CRYSTAL:
More correctly lead glass: Metal made with oxide of lead as the flux. True "Cut" and Crystal glass. Characterized by bell like tone when held by the base and lightly tapped with pencil or flicked (lightly) with fingernail. Heavier than other glass.

CULLETT
Broken Glass used for the sake of economy and to help fusing. It was sometimes cheaper to purchase broken glass than the ingredients from which the glass was made. Cullet also provided a saving of heat required to melt the batch. A certain percentage was added to every batch.

FINISHER:
He removed the mould marks from the upper sections of bowls, goblets, pitchers, etc.; a master craftsman.

FLINT:
Late-nineteenth and twentieth century description for any clear, colourless glass.

FLINT:
Glass of lead (flint glass) composed of sand, potash and oxide of lead, sometimes saltpetre was added and oxide of maganese was added to clear the colour and produce the crystal clearness. This glass became most desirable as quality glass. Previously it

Modern bottles which are appearing on store shelves and at flea markets without labels — attractive, but better value if purchased at regular prices with contents.

was believed that such fine glass could only be attained by using silica made from powdered flints (Crystal Glass). Glass termed "Flint" since the late nineteenth century is in fact usually "lime glass". William Leighton of Hobbs, Bruckunier and Company, Wheeling, U.S.A., used bicarbonate of soda, different proportions of lime and other ingredients until he hit on a formula that produced a truly clear glass, almost as bright as lead, not so heavy and having less resonance. This was a tremendous boost to the glass industry for now they were able to produce the look of quality without the cost. The student of glass looks at all pieces with a critical eye and becomes expert enough to tell the difference. Most of what is termed "flint" is in fact "lime" glass. Even some of those pieces so described in the Royal Ontario Museum, Toronto.

Much of the earlier glass made by both American and Canadian factories was the true - glass of lead or "flint" and it is an added thrill to the collector when he finds forms in the pattern or patterns he collects are "flint". Many patterns were made in both "flint" and "lime". If an example in "lime" turns up in a pattern previously considered essentially a "flint" product the authenticity should be checked.

Prices vary according to demand therefore it is not always the quality of the glass that establishes the price but the rarity.

FRIT:
Partially cooked and fused ingredients saved and added to a batch.

GATHER:
Molten glass removed from the batch at the gathering end of a blowpipe.

GLASS:
An artificial compound which is produced by the fusion of silica in the form of sand, flint or quartz, this is done with the aid of an alkaline flux, usually soda or potash. These are the essential ingredients but to produce durable glass, small amounts of other ingredients are added, lime or one of the oxides of lead.

LEHR (Leer):
Oven for tempering or annealing glassware.

LIME GLASS:
Glass made with soda and lime as a flux, the formula first discovered in 1864. Clear non-lead glass of some brilliance but little resonance.

MARVER:
Polished metal or stone slab on which the gather of glass is rolled.

METAL:
Glassmakers term for glass in molten or finished state.

POTASH:
It is today commercially prepared but early glass makers produced it by burning bracken or beechwood.

SODA:
Today made from common salt, previously from the ash of certain marine plants.

WHIMSEY:
An object made to demonstrate the skill of the glass blower. Non-commercial objects created for pleasure not profit.

CASE BOTTLES

The case bottle or "square face gin" bottle as it is known in England was first used by the Dutch to bottle their Geneva for export. The first of the bottles were packed in cases of twelve. It was found that the shape was easier to pack than any other and that less breakage resulted en route.

The bottle is found in various sizes and colours: clear, opal, milk and amber have been reported, but usually case bottles are very dark, some so dark as to be termed black.

The earliest Dutch Geneva bottles are slightly longer than the later case style and have a seal on the shoulder on which will be found initials or a crest. A. Van Hoboken of Rotterdam exported to the Americas and used the initials A.H. in this way.

Canadian makers of "Geneva" gin also use case bottles and have done so for many years, many of these bottles being produced by the Dominion Glass Company and having the D in Diamond trade mark.

Above — Case bottle re-used for wine. There were a number of wine makers in the Niagara area during the nineteenth and early twentieth century. Bottles were costly, so any useful size came in handy and was filled and given the appropriate label.

Right —
Three sizes of Canadian case bottles.

GLOSSARY
2

APPLIED LIP:
Mouth formed by adding glass strip to sheared lip of bottle after it has been taken from the blow pipe. Pre-1900.

APOTHECARY:
Druggist who prescribed and prepared drugs.

A.B.M.:
Automatic Bottle Machine. Bottles made by this machine are complete and have seam mark from top to bottom, also mold marks on base. First fully automated machine was the Owens. The Dominion Glass Co. of Canada used automatic bottle machines after 1903.

BATTLEDORE:
Wooden paddle used by blower in shaping bottle during the blowing process.

B.I.M.:
Blown in Mold, a combination of mold and hand finishing, not automated.

BITTERS:
Medication popular in the 19th century for which preposterous claims were made. It contained large amounts of alcohol which were disguised with herbs and other ingredients. Many of the medicine men concocted bitters under various names. Burdock's Blood Bitters was possibly the favorite in Canada.

BLACK GLASS:
Glass made with iron content, pre-1875.

BLOB TOP:
Thick heavy blob mouth used on the early soda water and mineral water bottles, also on pottery ginger beer and shandy bottles.

BLOW OVER:
Term used for seam left round shoulders of bottle which has been made in dip mold. This is caused by the expansion of glass over the top of the mold.

CARBOY:
See Jeroboam.

CASE BOTTLE:
Square faced bottle used to facilitate packing, originally used for "Geneva" Dutch Gin.

CHAIR:
Bench at which the "gaffer" sits whilst finishing glass work.

CLOSURE:
Descriptive term for anything used to seal a bottle.

Right —
Four types
of closure.

Left to right —
Glass stopper
with cork liner.
Cobb Stopper.
Internal thread.
Lightening Stopper.

Below —
Closures and
prices from
Hutchinson's
1912 catalogue.

Porcelain Stoppers

		Per Gross
Plain, complete		$1 75
Lettered, " in one color		2 00
" " less than 25 gross, charge for die.		
Buttons and Rubbers, plain		1 45
" " " lettered		1 70
Red Rubber Discs for Porcelain Stoppers		80

Beer Stoppers

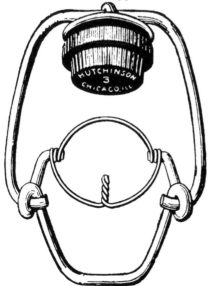

Send at least two sample bottles to insure proper fit.

Wire Cork Fasteners

SIZES.
ooooo ½ pint Apollinaris.
oooo Pint   "
ooo Quart   "
oo Extra size, seldom used.
o ⎫ 8-oz. or 28-oz. soda bot-
1 ⎬ tles according to neck fin-
2 ⎭ ish, ½ pt. and qt. bottles.
3 Round bottom bottles, imported.
4 Extra size, seldom used.
5 Extra size, seldom used.

Any size, price per gross $0 22
100 gross or more, per gross 20
Neck Wires, per gross 10
We recommend sending a sample bottle to insure perfect fit.

Center Twist Loops

Center Twist Loops, tinned, per M $0 35
Center Twist Loops, tinned, lots of 5 M 30

Ginger Ale Loops

Tinned No. 23 wire, per M $0 30

CODD STOPPER:
Type of closure which includes the use of a glass marble inside the neck of the bottle.

CUP BOTTOM MOLD:
Full height mold with cup indentation on the bottom plate.

DEMI—JOHN:
See Jeroboam.

DESERT GLASS:
See Suncast Amethyst.

EMBOSSED:
Bottle or jar with raised name or/and trade mark. It is estimated that something like 80% of bottles found have no embossing.

FIRE POLISHED:
Bottle reheated to give smoother finish and obliterate seams and tool marks.

FREE BLOWN:
Bottle blown and shaped without the use of molds. Every bottle has individuality and no two are exactly alike. There are no seams on free blown bottles.

FRUIT JAR:
Sometimes called Canning Jar, Sealer or Preserve Jar, a glass container made to hold and preserve food.

GAFFER:
Master blower, in charge of shop.

GATHERER:
One who gathers the glass.

GLASSHOUSE:
Works or factory where glass is made.

GLORY HOLE:
Small furnace used for reheating glass during blowing and finishing.

GRAPHITE PONTIL:
Term used to describe mark left by use of solid iron bar pontil rod.

GROUND PONTIL:
Mark left after jagged pontil has been ground off.

HAND BLOWN:
Bottle formed with the use of mold as well as blowing, not automatic.

INSIDE SCREW STOPPER:
Closure used with bottle having thread inside bottle mouth.

JEROBOAM:
Large sphere shaped bottle which will hold one to ten gallons.

KICK —UP:
See Push-up.

Old Time Bar

Photograph taken at Historic Fort Steele, B.C.

MARBLE STOPPER:
See Codd Stopper.

MELTING POT:
Clay pot in which batch is melted.

MOLD BLOWN:
See Hand Blown.

PARISON:
The inflated gather of glass.

PIECE MOLD:
Mold made of several sections which join up to make complete mold.

PUSH — UP:
Also called Kick-Up. Describes the hummock formed when base of bottle is pushed up to prevent rocking.

STRAP SIDE:
Ribs of glass one quarter to one half inch inch wide going up both sides of the bottle, width and thickness depand on size of bottle.

SUNCAST AMETHYST:
Describes glass which has changed colour after having been exposed to the sun. It only happens to glass made prior to 1915, which had Manganese Oxide added to the mixture from which it was made. This is sometimes called 'desert glass'.

SUNCAST YELLOW or STRAW:
Glass coloured by the sun, but to which Selenium had been added in the making, 1916 — 1930. The depth of colour in either case is dependent on the amount of chemical added and the length of time exposed to the sun.

TORPEDO BOTTLE:
Early soda water bottle with pointed rather than rounded base.

WHITTLE MARKS:
Marks caused by the blowing of the bottle in a cold mold. The marks are sometimes dimpled or hammered in appearance and on some bottles take the form of wavy lines.

Marks also appear on bottles made in the early wooden molds, these left a diamond like design on the glass when the mold was not dipped in water before use or had become too dry.

Lower Fort Garry, Big House Wet Larder. *Photograph courtesy Historic Sites Division.*

BIBLIOGRAPHY

Abbott, A.L.	*Old Bottles: How and Where to Find Them*	Abbott and Abbott, 1970.
Adams, J.P.	*Bottle Collecting in New England*	New Hampshire Publishing Company, 1969.
Adams, J.P.	*Bottle Collecting in America*	New Hampshire Publishing Company, 1971.
Austen, F.	*Poor Man's Guide to Bottle Collecting*	Doubleday and Company Inc., 1971.
Bates, V.T. and Chamberlain, B.	*Antique Bottle Finds in New England*	Noone House, 1968.
Bird, D. and M. & Corke, C.	*A Century of Antique Canadian Fruit Jars*	Authors, London, Ont., 1970.
Blumenstein, L.	*Bottle Rush U.S.A.*	Old Time Bottle Publishing Company, 1969.
Blumenstein, L.	*Old Time Bottles Found in Ghost Towns*	Old Time Bottle Publishing Company, 1969.
Denison, Merrill	*The Barley & The Stream*	McClelland & Stewart Ltd., 1955.
Hotchkiss, J. & Cassidy, J.	*Bottle Collecting Manual With Prices*	Hotchkiss House, 1971.
Kendrick, Grace	*The Antique Bottle Collector*	Edwards Brothers Inc., 1963.
Munsey, C.	*The Illustrated Guide to Collecting Bottles*	Hawthorn Books, 1970.
Phillips, H.V.	*Antique Bottles*	Logan Print, 1967.
Revi, A.C.	*American Pressed Glass and Figure Bottles*	Thomas Nelson & Sons, 1962.
Stevens, Gerald	*Canadian Glass c. 1825 — 1925*	Ryerson Press, Toronto 1967.
Toulouse, J.H.	*Bottle Makers and Their Marks*	Thomas Nelson Inc., 1971.
Toulouse, J.H.	*Fruit Jars*	Thomas Nelson Inc., 1969.
Umberger, J. & A.L.	*Collectible Character Bottles*	Corker Book Company, 1969.
Unitt, Doris & Peter	*Treasury of Canadian Glass*	Clock House, Peterborough, Ontario, 1969.
Vienneau, A.	*The Bottle Collector*	Petheric Press, 1969.
Yount, J.T.	*Bottle Collector's Handbook and Pricing Guide*	Educator Books, 1970.

Also almanacs, directories, magazines and newspapers from 1825 — 1935.